girls

without limits

Dedication

Susan Jones Sears, PhD
1940–2012

You saw potential in me that I did not see in myself. Thank you for paving the way for an entire generation of women and girls. You were a trailblazer, a teacher, a mentor, and friend.

I miss you.

girls
without limits

helping girls achieve **healthy relationships,**
academic success, and **interpersonal strength**

lisa hinkelman

CORWIN
A SAGE Company

CORWIN
A SAGE Company

FOR INFORMATION

Corwin
A SAGE Company
2455 Teller Road
Thousand Oaks, California 91320
(800) 233–9936
www.corwin.com

SAGE Publications Ltd.
1 Oliver's Yard
55 City Road
London, EC1Y 1SP
United Kingdom

SAGE Publications India Pvt. Ltd.
B 1/I 1 Mohan Cooperative Industrial Area
Mathura Road, New Delhi 110 044
India

SAGE Publications Asia-Pacific Pte. Ltd.
3 Church Street
#10-04 Samsung Hub
Singapore 049483

Acquisitions Editor: Jessica Allan
Associate Editor: Julie Nemer
Editorial Assistant: Lisa Whitney
Production Editor: Amy Schroller
Copy Editor: Kimberly Hill
Typesetter: Hurix Systems Private Ltd.
Proofreader: Eleni-Maria Georgiou
Indexer: Maria Sosnowski
Cover Designer: Gail Buschman
Permissions Editor: Karen Ehrmann

Printed in the United States of America

A catalog record of this book is available from the Library of Congress.

ISBN 9781452241210

This book is printed on acid-free paper.

MIX
Paper from
responsible sources
FSC
www.fsc.org
FSC® C014174

13 14 15 16 17 10 9 8 7 6 5 4 3 2 1

Contents

Preface

As I began to think about how best to study and work with girls, I was not sure where to start, nor was I sure where this research would lead me. I poured through scholarly research articles, books, and newspaper stories directed toward issues facing girls. I attended conferences and professional development trainings where counselors, psychologists, and educators discussed the "girl crisis." Strategies were offered to increase the self-esteem of girls, expose girls to more diverse careers, and encourage girls to be anything that they wanted to be. But I quickly realized that the best starting place was to actually talk to girls and really listen to what they had to say! I wanted to understand what is going on in girls' lives, in their own words. I wanted to understand why the adolescent years feel so tumultuous and lonely for girls and why they consistently report feeling that they aren't quite good enough.

The research in this book took place over a period of nearly eight years. My research team and I have surveyed and interviewed thousands of girls from different backgrounds, ethnicities, socioeconomic statuses, and ages. We have talked with girls who are incarcerated, who are homeless, who live in middle-class homes, and who live in mansions. We learned from girls who are in two-parent families, foster care, single-parent families, divorced families, and who live with their grandparents. We spent time listening to girls in very poor urban schools, middle-class suburban schools, elite independent schools, and low-income rural schools. Girls in public, parochial, private, and charter schools participated in our research and shared their thoughts, feelings, and opinions with us. We provided them with a safe place to talk, and did not pass judgment. We just listened.

What we learned is that there are vast differences among girls in regards to their experiences, their thoughts, and their opinions. Girls' knowledge of various topics is based upon the environment where they are raised. Depending upon what they have been exposed to, girls' perceptions of the opportunities available to them can vary greatly. But the one thing that continued to amaze me as I talked with more and more girls was that the fundamental issues that are facing girls are much more universal than they are different. While girls can have extremely different experiences based upon their socioeconomic status, race and ethnicity, family composition, or ability, I have found that the experience of girlhood, while unique for every girl, looks amazingly similar for girls across the country. Despite the vast differences between and among girls, the commonalities and shared experiences strongly outweigh the differences. Negotiating friendships and fitting in, experiencing insecurity about one's body, managing dating relationships and sexual pressure, and dealing with the social, emotional, and cognitive changes of adolescence seem to be universal issues for many American teen girls. Girls are under pressure and are at-risk for negative outcomes simply because they are female. Girls are more likely than boys to: dislike their body, be on a diet, feel pressure to look sexy, experience sexual violence, have low self-esteem, experience depression, and attempt suicide.

Despite these challenges, we know that girls are strong and resilient. They consistently exceed the limited expectations that are placed upon them by society and the media and they continue to amaze and inspire us. We also know that girls are better able to fully realize their potential when they have caring adults in their lives who nurture, challenge, encourage, and support them.

My goal in writing this book is to give a voice to girls who often feel that their thoughts and opinions are unheard and devalued. There are so many professionals, psychologists, teachers, and authors who have been telling us what girls want, what girls need, and what we should do with the girls in our lives, but few have taken the time to survey and talk to thousands of girls from many backgrounds. I wanted to know: What's going through girls' minds? What do they dream about? What fills them with insecurity? What do they think are the big things going on in their lives that adults don't understand? And ultimately, what can we do to help them? I want to provide adults with a glimpse into the lives of girls, as described by the girls themselves, and offer concrete strategies for how adults can better understand, communicate with, and motivate the girls in their lives.

I recognize that this book does not address the unique issues that face every girl. For example, our research did not directly address some of the social, emotional, and developmental issues that face girls–such as sexual orientation and gender identity, spirituality, specific developmental or learning issues, drug and alcohol use and abuse, nor pregnancy and teen parenting. However, it does offer a perspective on the shared experiences of girls, and the ways that, because of their gender, all girls can experience limitations and decreased expectations in life.

Our role as caring adults in the lives of girls is to understand these challenges and equip girls with the skills to effectively navigate their adolescent years and construct a life that is full of purpose, meaning, pride, and fulfillment. We want girls to perceive their options as infinite and their abilities as expandable, and we each have a role in helping girls construct a life without limits.

Acknowledgments

While this book has been a dream of mine for many years, I fully recognize that any endeavor such as this does not happen without the support and encouragement of many others. I have been blessed to have wonderful family, friends, colleagues, and students in my life that share my commitment to girls and who have contributed their time and talent in profound ways to help this project come to fruition.

My Grandma Irene was one of the first people in my life who truly demonstrated how women can step outside the box, push back against societal expectations, and live a full, rich, and happy life. She helped inspire my initial work with girls and women, and, although she has been gone for quite some time, her spirit continues to motivate me. How proud she would be to see the ideas that we discussed over pots of coffee in her kitchen come to fruition in a book that is focused on helping girls be limitless!

My husband, Bob Heine, has, without fail, been my constant and unwavering support. Giving me lots of space, patience, and understanding—he has set the bar for what a supportive, loving spouse and friend should be. Knowing when to comfort and take care of me and when to leave me alone to my own thoughts and musings, he has truly been my partner and rock throughout this crazy journey. I am blessed and lucky to have him in my life and do not know how I would have completed this project without him. He's the best!

My parents, Rich and Joan Hinkelman, instilled in me an early sense that girls can do and be anything that they want. Ensuring that I would not be limited or restricted by my gender, my parents supported my athletic, academic, and career aspirations for as long as I can remember. From throwing those 100 softball pitches every day with my dad in the yard to learning how to make a killer apple cake from my mother, I was afforded the opportunity to be affirmed for being both strong and feminine. I never had to decide whether or not I "shouldn't" be good at something because I was a girl or that I "should" be good at other things because I was a girl. My parents celebrated my individuality and encouraged creativity and risk taking. Being strong was as important as being sensitive, and taking care of myself was equally as important as taking care of others. Their ongoing prayers and support have sustained me and it is my sincere hope that little girls everywhere have the opportunity to grow up with parents who give their daughters the gift of confidence and sense of limitlessness that my parents gave me.

My brother, Richard Hinkelman, has been the most amazing and supportive brother anyone could ask for. He has shown me unconditional love, ridiculous humor, and, when needed, appropriate challenge. Richard is the person who you call in the middle of the night when your computer crashes, when you do not have one more creative word left in your body, and when you question whether any of your work matters. He provides reassurance, a funny anecdote, and the motivation to persevere. His deep convictions, commitment to social justice, and love and compassion for others are a constant reminder to me that, while there is much work to be done, we are each responsible for doing our part to care for others and to add value to the world. I am so proud to be his sister and am grateful for our amazing relationship.

I want to extend my sincere thanks and gratitude to my friend and colleague, Deborah Schipper. Deb was one of the first people that I met during my initial graduate studies, and she was extremely influential in helping shape and focus the course of my life's work. Her passion for, and commitment to, the safety of girls and women extends into all aspects of her life. As a professional women's self-defense instructor, Deb has taught thousands of girls and women physical self-defense and she believes wholeheartedly in a girl's ability to successfully defend herself from violence. Deb works to ensure that every girl and woman she works with also comes to believe this about herself. Deb's feedback, editing, and consistent encouragement helped make this project seem manageable and achievable, and her bravery, honesty, and courage have inspired me to take risks and conquer seemingly insurmountable challenges.

My colleagues and friends, Dr. Michelle Bruno and Lauren Hancock, have served as creative, moral, academic, and social support throughout this entire process. Providing hundreds of hours of data entry, transcription, and analysis, they have contributed a great deal to our deep understanding of the issues impacting girls. With a shared commitment to girls, equity, and access to education, these ladies have been the validation of my reality for many years. They provided friendship and encouragement as well as ongoing comic relief. They have been patient, flexible, creative, loving, and supportive. Our friendship has reiterated to me the importance, value, and strength in female bonds and I am grateful for their push for more moderation in my life. Every girl needs friends like Michelle and Lauren who will help lift them up, support and encourage them, reframe their setbacks, soothe their hurts, and celebrate their successes.

So many other folks have helped this project in large and small ways. From offering a writing retreat, to providing substantive and practical feedback on my ideas, to offering legal and professional advice, to keeping me sane and entertained, I am richly blessed by friends and colleagues who help sustain me. A heartfelt and sincere thanks to Jessica Allen, Maureen Casamassimo, Laura Comek, Esq., Dr. Patricia Cunningham, Michael Matalka, Loren McKeon, Tammy Roberts Myers, Dr. Melissa Ockerman, and all my friends at Premium.

I have also been blessed to work with a wonderful group of graduate students, school counselors, and ROX facilitators. These ladies have given of their time and tremendous talent to positively impact the lives of thousands of girls. They have delivered programming, assisted with data collection, and have been the amazing role models that young girls need in their lives. I am grateful for their ongoing commitment to girls and their willingness to make a substantial and sustainable impact in the lives of each girl that they work with.

A final thank you to all the parents, teachers, counselors, administrators, and especially girls who have taken the time to talk with me over the last several years about their thoughts, opinions, and experiences. Without you, none of this work would have been possible. I have been amazed at the willingness of people to share their personal experiences with me and have been honored to hear the stories and thoughts of thousands of girls. It is my hope that through sharing their stories with you, you are able to understand not only the challenges that girls face but also recognize the strength, potential, and promise in today's generation of girls. These girls are the future, let's help them succeed!

PUBLISHER'S ACKNOWLEDGMENTS

Corwin gratefully acknowledges the contributions of the following reviewers:

Scott Currier
Mathematics Teacher
Nute High School
Milton, NH

Terri Hadley
School Counselor
Dunlap Middle School
Dunlap, IL

Connie Hanel
Academic Achievement Specialist
Medaille College
Buffalo, NY

Robin E. Ruiz
Professional Educator Leader
PCSB, Denison Middle School
Winter Haven, FL

Dr. Marilyn Steneken
Science Teacher
Sparta Middle School
Sparta, NJ

About the Author

 **Dr. Lisa Hinkelman** is the Founder and Director of Ruling Our eXperiences, Inc. (ROX), a 501(c)(3) nonprofit organization that delivers evidence-based empowerment programming to girls (www.rulingourexperiences.com). Started in 2006 in Columbus, Ohio, ROX has grown to a regionally operated organization with thousands of participants in urban, suburban, rural, and parochial schools. ROX is focused on equipping girls with the information and skills necessary to live healthy, independent, and violence-free lives.

Hinkelman has spent years working with girls, parents, and educators in both educational and counseling settings and has been aggressively researching the experiences of diverse girls for the past seven years. She consults regularly for schools, organizations, and agencies on the critical issues impacting girls, bullying and relational aggression, child abuse and violence prevention, and other social, emotional, safety, and mental health issues facing students and schools. As a licensed professional counselor, Dr. Hinkelman also operates Equip Your Mind, LLC, a counseling, consulting, research, and evaluation practice in Columbus, Ohio (www.equipyourmind.com).

Dr. Hinkelman is a graduate of Chatham College in Pittsburgh, Pennsylvania, where she earned her degrees in Psychology and Education. She additionally earned her MA and PhD in Counselor Education from the Ohio State University. She completed training in mental health counseling and school counseling and has served on the Counselor Education faculty at the Ohio State University since 2004, where she continues to teach

Counseling Children and Legal and Ethical Issues in Counseling. She has authored numerous publications, book chapters, articles, and educational curricula on topics, including self-esteem development, motivational interviewing, sexual violence prevention, career exploration, and study skills. Hinkelman can be reached at 614-488-8600 or lisahinkelman@rulingourexperiences.com.

CHAPTER 1

What's Really Going on for Girls and How Can We Help Them?

"I don't think that adults have any idea what our lives are really like. They think they know what is going on but they don't really. When I think about the big things going on for girls my age I think the first thing is girl drama. It is constant and never ending. Girls just look for ways to create drama and will make stuff up when everything is fine. Girls talk behind each other's backs and try to get certain girls to not like other girls. You just have to make sure that you are in with the 'right' girls so you don't get caught up in the middle of it all."

—Laci, seventh grade

The drama of girlhood. Is it a reality made up by girls who have too much time on their hands, or is it a necessary rite of passage that all girls experience? Do the issues that we see in the media greatly influence how girls see themselves, or have we overplayed the importance of popular culture in the lives of girls? What do girls like about being a girl? What frustrates girls about the adults in their lives? What are the big issues that girls are dealing with and what keeps them awake at night? And perhaps most importantly, how can we best support these young women?

These are the questions that I set out to answer nearly eight years ago when I began to research girls. I wanted to talk to girls and hear their perspectives and their realities, in their own words. I wanted to give a voice to girls who feel that sometimes their thoughts and opinions are overlooked.

As I talked to teachers, counselors, and parents, I learned that most adults are eager to help girls, but they often don't know where to start. They recognize that girls' lives are challenging but realize that they have difficulty relating and connecting to girls. The goal in this book is to give adults who work with and care about girls some insights into the lives of girls, as well as provide strategies for building relationships and working more effectively with girls.

In asking girls about the big things going on in their lives, lots of different topics emerged. Even among girls who live in close-knit families, attend high performing schools, and are involved in multiple extracurricular activities, they still report struggling with friendships, dating relationships, and body image concerns. They talked about pressure, issues in their families and their relationships with their parents, difficulty in friendships and dating relationships, tremendous pressures around weight and body image, and major concerns surrounding self-esteem and how they feel about themselves. They talked about puberty, academics, getting their driver's license, and dealing with depression and suicidal thoughts. But, overwhelmingly, the issues that girls talked the most about were clustered around a handful of topic areas, including friendships, drama, dating, weight and body image, and pressure. A consistent theme was that adults don't *really* understand what they are going through so girls have difficulty openly sharing their issues and concerns with the adults in their lives.

In talking with adults, many felt at a loss as to how they could develop more effective relationships with girls. Teachers reported frustration with girls "dumbing themselves down" around boys, counselors struggled with how to address the girl drama and bullying that is plaguing their schools, and parents felt anxiety regarding how they could best help their daughters deal with the increased pressures and challenges of middle school and high school.

What became increasingly obvious was that adults are hungry for information, strategies, and activities that they can use to connect with the girls in their lives. They want to find ways to help girls become the best that they can be and experience rich, fulfilling, and productive lives. When asked what girls need to be successful, overwhelmingly, teachers, administrators, counselors, and parents identified "confidence" as most important. They agree that girls' lack of confidence can hold them back; however, they are not sure how they can help build confidence in girls.

Arguably, how we feel about ourselves can impact nearly every decision that we make. Our sense of self-confidence and self-concept influences our decisions and can help determine the choices that we make in many facets of our lives, including our relationships, academic pursuits, and careers. If I am in an unhealthy dating relationship and I don't have a positive self-concept, I may stay in the relationship because I am afraid to leave and I don't think that I could do any better. If I lack confidence around my academic abilities, I may opt to take a general math course instead of trigonometry because I fear that I might not succeed. If I lack self-esteem, I may feel that I am not smart enough to be successful in my dream career, so I will compromise and pursue something less risky or less prestigious. How different could our decisions be if we moved through the world with confidence in ourselves and our abilities?

The self-esteem of girls drops as they go through their adolescent years (Biro, Striegel-Moore, & Franko, 2006; Pipher, 1994). There is a drop from elementary school to middle school, and then there is another drop from middle school on to high school. Girls often report they do not feel confident in themselves or comfortable in their changing bodies and can become withdrawn and unsure of themselves. Have you ever seen a rowdy group of fourth or fifth grade girls who are loud and laughing without a care in the world, then when they hit seventh grade they become insecure and consumed with their looks, clothes, and potential dating partners? I recently had a ninth-grade girl tell me that the last time she felt confident and happy with her body was when she was in fourth grade.

During the childhood and adolescent years, girls are inundated with negative messages about, and unrealistic images of, females. As girls begin to develop an understanding of themselves and their environment, they are influenced by the messages that they receive from others. They can internalize these often negative and limiting messages and experience poor self-concept, dissatisfaction with their bodies, lowered expectations about their academic and career opportunities, increased acceptance of violence in relationships, and long-term self-esteem issues.

However, we also know that girls are brave, courageous, and resilient. They have the potential to make tough decisions, chart their personal goals, and control their own experiences. Girls can rise above the negative messages and influences that they are exposed to and construct a confident and strong sense of self. Our role is to help instill a sense of confidence and capability in girls so that they believe that they have the right to a happy and fulfilling life, and that they also have the support and skills to actually construct a life that they love.

HOW CAN WE HELP GIRLS?

"I don't understand these girls!"

"I have no idea how to talk to my daughter; she just rolls her eyes every time I say something."

"Girls today are way different from how they were when I was a teenager. . . . I just don't even know where to start."

These comments from educators, parents, and other adults illustrate that girls who were once open, communicative, and easy to understand have become confusing strangers, and adults feel paralyzed as to how to forge a new, or repair an existing, relationship with a girl.

While we might not always understand what is going on for girls, and we may have difficulty comprehending the way that they think and reason, there are many things that we can do to communicate care and concern to the girls in our lives. While the remainder of this book will delineate specific issues and topics that impact girls' lives, there are some general recommendations that can help us effectively make connections with, communicate with, and help the young ladies in our lives.

Those of us who work with youth know that, despite our best efforts, we are unable to control what is going on in their lives outside of our interactions with them. As educators, you know that girls may come to you with histories of abuse, violent home life, and a lack of supportive and caring adults. They may not have a bed to sleep in, food for breakfast, or clean clothes when they come to school. While we can at times feel frustrated and helpless, our role in these situations is to add positive and prosocial things to girls' lives. Research tells us that the more deficits, challenges, or barriers that girls have, the more positive supports we need to add to their lives (Bernard, 1993). We believe that our positive intervention can outweigh the impact of the negative factors in their lives.

We do this by communicating our care, our passion, and our genuine concern for the development and well-being of girls. We want to help girls identify and find their dreams. We want to help girls find their own happiness and be able to articulate what that looks like for them. What excites them? What fuels their passion? What do they care about? And how can we help them construct their lives to be fulfilling, passionate, and purposeful?

There are simple and concrete things that adults can do to connect with, care for, motivate, and support the girls in their lives.

#1: Be Aware

Be aware of what is going on in the lives of girls by paying attention to the things that they care about. Whether it is popular culture, music, news related to girls, media attention around girls and women, or the pressures that are facing girls, attempting to be relevant and knowledgeable can be helpful in creating an effective bond with the girls in your life. Girls report feeling that adults don't get them and don't understand what is happening in their lives. They feel that adults are far removed from the actual challenges that they face and that it's nearly impossible for adults to truly understand what it is like to be a girl today.

Maintaining an awareness of the things girls care about can mean paying attention to the relevant and contemporary issues facing girls. For example, recognizing how the media and culture inform and influence girls: Who are the hottest musicians, the famous actors on the posters in their rooms, the latest books and movies, and the modern athletes and teen idols? This does not mean that we overemphasize the importance of media and popular culture, but rather we demonstrate to girls that we care about what is going on in their lives and, at least in some small way, have an understanding of what is "cool." Of course, we don't have to actually *agree* that anyone or anything is cool, but we need to know what the girls think is cool.

You might make a habit of tuning in to popular reality shows while cleaning the house, leafing through magazines while checking out at the grocery store, and listening to different types of music while driving in your car. Does this mean that you are into reality TV, gossip magazines, or Top 40 music? Not necessarily. It just means that you are trying to stay connected to what girls are exposed to on a daily basis.

Assess your own knowledge of contemporary girl culture:

1. Who are the top "hot" musicians right now?

2. What is the current "must see" movie for teen girls?

3. What is the social media platform or network of choice for girls?

4. What apps, computer programs, and games are girls currently interested in?

5. What would girls say they like to do in their spare time?

6. Who are the "it" actors and actresses in Hollywood?

While it is important to attempt to understand the realities of girls' lives, it is equally important to maintain the appropriate relationship with the girls in your life. And that brings us to our second strategy:

#2: Be the Adult

A caring adult does not take on the role of a friend or a peer. Often, we see adults who work with girls seek to be a friend to the girls rather than maintaining an appropriate adult-teen relationship. This is one incidence where the attempt to be knowledgeable and relevant can go too far. As adults, we are not the contemporaries of the girls in our lives, and we do not want to send confusing messages to them.

A middle school principal shared a story about one of her seventh grade student's mothers who was very intent on being the "cool mom." She wanted to be the mom that all the other girls would come to and with whom they could gossip about other kids. This particular mother was overinvolved in the girls' lives and took great pride in being the person that the other girls could share their secrets with.

Where the situation went from mildly uncomfortable to slightly more inappropriate was when the mom would get upset if she wasn't invited to be part of the girls' conversations when they had sleepovers at her house. She admitted to hiding on the staircase and listening in on the girls' discussions, because she felt left out when the girls retreated to the basement game room for private conversations. When her own daughter turned to the school counselor to share her concerns and talk about her problems, the mother became very distressed and angry with the school counselor. Mom was frustrated and upset that her daughter did not want to tell her the things that were bothering her but would rather seek out the listening ear of another caring adult in her daughter's life.

There is a fine line between being relevant and understanding in the life of girls and trying to relive your teen years through your kids or students. We must ensure that we maintain a healthy balance of relevance coupled with appropriate boundaries. We don't want to make things confusing for the girls by requiring them to discern what the relationship boundaries should be. So while it is important that we stay informed and connected, it is probably less important and would even be embarrassing for the girls if we blurred the boundaries between adult and peer.

#3: Start the Conversation

One of the most important ways that we can help girls is to be the one to start the conversation and then work to maintain open lines of communication. Sometimes, however, starting the conversation can be difficult, particularly if that has been a challenge for us in the past. Communication can ultimately dictate the success or failure of any relationship, and often a hallmark of the adolescent years is a decrease in the effective communication between adults and teens.

Our goal in communicating with girls is to make them feel that what they have to share with us is valuable and important and that they are the most important person in our lives at any given time. We start the conversation by inviting girls to share with us what is going on in their lives and then really listen to what they have to say.

We demonstrate our interest, care, and concern by genuinely seeking to understand the other person's reality. It always feels good when another person truly wants to understand how we feel, what our experience has been, and how we make sense of a situation without seeking to impose their own beliefs on the situation. This type of listening, is listening to *understand,* not listening to *respond.* When we are truly seeking to understand someone else's experiences, thoughts, and feelings, we invite the disclosure from their own space, without seeking to impose our beliefs or our judgment on them. When we do this, other people feel safe and comfortable in the relationship. They know that they won't be judged and they know that their feelings won't be deemed as silly or inappropriate.

Here are some ways to start an open conversation that allows the girl to decide what to talk about:

- Tell me about yourself.
- Share with me something of which you are especially proud.
- Tell me more about that.
- I don't know a lot about that. . . . It would be great if you could explain it to me.
- I saw _____ on TV last night. What do you think of him/her/it?
- Wow, that situation seems pretty tough. . . . Tell me how you are dealing with it.
- What do you think about _____?

As you can tell, different situations call for different types of communication, but creating a safe and open space for dialogue must be an intentional activity on our part. Sometimes this means that we have to monitor our own language, tone of voice, and communication patterns, and then intentionally reframe our responses.

#4: Reframe the Response

Our communication styles can sometimes unintentionally raise defenses and shut down the dialogue. To open up the lines of conversation requires an effort on our part that I call reframing the response. When we reframe our responses, we pay attention to what we might *normally* say to girls in a particular situation and we catch ourselves and reframe what we *actually* say. Sometimes our initial responses can sound judgmental or patronizing and can serve to stifle the conversation. If our responses are not perceived as judgment but rather as an attempt to understand, how much more productive could our communication actually be?

When we reframe our response, we must first monitor our own communication style. How often do we say things that others could perceive as snippy, judgmental, or paternalistic? Are we more likely to say, "Do you seriously think you are going to wear that outfit out of this house?" or "Honey, I am not sure if that outfit is the best choice for this event. Let's think about this together." Despite what we may actually be thinking, when we control our nonverbal messages (i.e., the expressions on our face, what we do with our eyes, if we look angry, surprised, disgusted, etc.) as well as our verbal messages (i.e., the tone and content of what actually comes out of our mouths) our chances of increasing communication and keeping a more open dialogue improve.

For example, if you say the following to a teen who may have recently made a poor decision, "Now, tell me, did you think that that was a good idea?" you can fairly easily guess what the response will be. Asking a question in this way only serves to suppress the conversation and probably completely shut it down. If we instead say, "Share with me a bit about what you were thinking and what was going on for you when this happened," we might get a very different response. Obviously our inflection and tone of voice matter when we communicate, but the actual words that we say matter as well. Consider the following:

Example #1:

- *Option 1:* "Did you see Lady Gaga on the MTV Awards show last night? She is so crazy and wears the most ridiculous outfits. I don't get how people think she has any talent at all. What do you think about her?"

- *Option 2:* "What did you think about Lady Gaga's performance on the MTV Awards show last night?"

Example #2:

- *Option 1:* "Your teacher told me that you haven't been turning in your homework and I would like an explanation right now."

- *Option 2:* "I'm wondering if you have been having some trouble with your math homework. Your teacher shared some concerns with me and I wanted to check in with you."

Which statements do you think would encourage a girl to open up to you, help her believe that her opinions matter, and feel that you are a safe person to talk with about her problems?

#5: Communicate Care and Concern

One of the most important things we can do in the lives of girls is to communicate that we care and that we are concerned. Research tells us that there is perhaps no stronger predictor of success in a child's life than the legitimate and genuine care and concern from even just one adult (Bernard, 1993). Caring and support are building blocks of resiliency, but for some girls, it may be difficult for them to identify even one adult who cares deeply for them.

When you think back on your adolescent years, who was the person, or persons, who cared deeply for you? Who held high expectations for you and ensured that you succeeded? Who was the person that you could rely on who would never let you down?

Some girls can identify a lengthy list of these caring adults in their life, and other girls have difficulty coming up with even one name. Obviously, you are reading this book because you care about girls and have young ladies in your life. You know the person that you pictured when you were posed the aforementioned questions. I believe that our goal is for girls to picture us when they are asked those very same questions.

How you can show that you care:

Pay attention to the things that are
important to her and follow up accordingly.

This could mean asking how her softball tournament went over the weekend, how her family is adjusting to having a new baby brother in the house, or how the visit went with her grandparents over the holidays. This shows that you listen, pay attention, and that you care.

Look for opportunities to connect her
to positive people and activities.

Girls flourish when they have meaningful and positive connections in their lives. Unfortunately, we are observing a generation of teens who are becoming more socially isolated and who see their main sources of socialization and entertainment as connecting with peers online and via social media. Getting girls involved with people and activities that will build them up, challenge them, support them, and encourage them is key in building resilient girls. Some ideas include the following: church youth groups, sports teams, volunteer opportunities, neighborhood clean ups, mission or service trips, book clubs, science camps, art classes, hiking and nature camps, martial arts, ice skating, scrapbooking events, and music lessons. National organizations where girls can connect with other girls as well as with caring adults may include Girl Scouts, Big Brothers/Big Sisters, Boys and Girls Clubs, Girls Incorporated, Ruling Our Experiences, Inc. (ROX), and the YWCA. Research the local organizations or activities in your community that offer programming and opportunities for girls.

Spend time rather than money.

I work with a 13-year-old girl, Natalie, who is having trouble getting along with her parents. They are constantly bickering and both the teen and the parents are frustrated. Taking a solution-focused approach, I asked Natalie to share with me what is happening when she and her mom are getting along. What are the things that *she* is doing, and what are the things that *her mom* is doing? Natalie said, "When she buys me stuff we get along." Later, when I talked to Natalie's mom about the same topic, mom agreed that she often bought things for Natalie because she was constantly looking for what would make her daughter happy and encourage her daughter to be nice to her. Unfortunately, this strategy backfired because Natalie has begun to associate her mother's affection with shopping and buying new things, and as Natalie gets older, mom is continually trying to buy bigger and more expensive things to show her daughter her love. Thus, Natalie is getting spoiled, and the mom-daughter relationship is not improving. Building a relationship around shared interests and quality time together creates meaningful and sustainable bonds, whereas basing interactions on more superficial factors can equate to fewer authentic exchanges.

#6: Set Goals and Expect Success

It is possible to be caring and supportive, while also holding high expectations for girls. We want girls to be successful. We want them to have success in their relationships, friendships, academic pursuits, and career decision making. We want girls to envision a successful life for themselves and hold themselves to high expectations of performance and achievement.

As discussed previously, there can be situations where girls perceive the expectations that parents and others place on them as unrealistic and stressful. When this occurs, girls can internalize this desire to please others and become stressed-out and perfectionistic. Having high expectations and holding girls to achieving their expectations is an important goal, as well as a delicate balance. We want girls to believe in themselves but also know that we believe in them. Holding high expectations for girls communicates to them that we believe that they are capable of achieving at a high level and that we will support them in getting there.

We can support girls in achieving their dreams by helping them set goals. Goal setting is a very purposeful and concrete activity, and when done correctly can make even the largest task feel manageable. For nearly every topic addressed in this book, the activity of setting goals can be incorporated. I have used the following exercise to address academic performance, career development, healthy behavior, physical activity, and have even used it with two people to identify ways that they can make improvements in their relationship.

Too often, we set goals that are vague, unrealistic, and unattainable. For goals to be appropriately motivating they need to be specific, but they also must be *both* challenging and realistic. A common strategy for goal setting is using the SMART goal framework. While you may see various iterations of the acronym, SMART goals are:

Specific: Identify what it is precisely that you want to accomplish. A goal has a much greater chance of being achieved if it is specific and well articulated rather than vague or general.

Measurable: Determine how you will measure progress on the goal and use a concrete metric to monitor the progress. This will help you celebrate small successes and will keep you on track.

Attainable: Goals should be appropriately challenging but also attainable. Goals that are too easy to achieve tend to not require much motivation or focus—we can easily get bored. Conversely, goals that are far out of reach can seem unwieldy and we can become easily frustrated and can give up.

Relevant: Goals must be based on the actual realities of your life and take into consideration the environment, climate, and the "givens" of a situation. They should be meaningful and significant and make a difference in *your* life. If a goal does not feel relevant to the person (but rather is a goal that someone else is setting for them), there is little motivation to achieve. I, personally, have to see the goal as important and relevant to my life if I am going to work hard to achieve it!

Time-Sensitive: Include a timeline when setting a goal because it can help ensure that the task will get completed. This can mean that a student has nine weeks to improve her grade in science or that she will learn how to play a challenging arrangement on the piano in time for the recital that is two months away. Goals can have relatively short timelines (a few weeks) or long timelines (over the course of years). Working up against a deadline can keep us engaged and motivated.

There are many ways to use a goal-setting activity such as this. Having girls think about goals that are important to them and then helping them translate their ideas into SMART goals is an initial step. Next, it is important to help girls identify the activities and supports that will help them achieve their goals. What will they have to do to make progress on their goals? What are the behaviors they will have to engage in and what are the resources and supports they will need to achieve?

> **Example:**
> • General Goal: I will improve my physical fitness.
> • SMART Goal: I will work out at the gym three days a week for the next six months. I will do cardiovascular exercises two days a week and strength training one day a week.

To set the SMART goal above, I need to have access to a gym that has cardio and weight training equipment. I need to have transportation to the gym, and I need to be able to fit three days a week into my schedule. Considering the realities of the situation can help us set goals that are realistic and achievable.

#7: Encourage Risk Taking

Encouraging risk taking does not mean encouraging girls to engage in risky behavior; rather, it means encouraging girls to push themselves beyond their own perceptions of their capabilities. Risk taking allows girls the opportunity to see themselves as being able to achieve more than they thought possible. We want to instill in girls the sense that if they try something new, they may fail or they may develop an entire new set of competencies and skills. Examples include trying out for the school play, running for student government, standing up to a bully, taking an Advanced Placement (AP) course, or joining a sports team. Risk taking means putting oneself in a situation where success is not a sure thing. While it can be difficult and painful to watch those that we love struggle at certain things, we are helping prepare them for life's ups and downs. We recognize our need to keep our girls protected and well-insulated from the dangers of the world; however, when we help instill a strong sense of self in a girl, she is more apt to "stick her neck out" and try something that she may have been less inclined to try if she had lower self-confidence.

We want girls to know that the only regret we do not want them to have is the regret of not doing something because they feared failure. Girls need to know how to experience both success and failure and be prepared to effectively and graciously manage both. Encourage them to get out there and try something new—and be there to support them regardless of the outcome!

#8: Don't Just Set Limits, Teach Skills

We know that girls will deal with pressures, negative influences, and difficult situations. They will find themselves in predicaments that will require them to trust their instincts and make good decisions. Our hope is that when girls are in such situations they have the wherewithal to make the right decision. We have an opportunity to help prepare girls by teaching them the actual skills they will need to use in tough situations.

Too often, our desire is to keep girls protected by imposing strict rules and limits for their behavior. No watching MTV, no attending parties with boys, no riding in cars with friends, no dating until you are 16, no listening to certain types of music, and no going to concerts. While rules, limits, and consequences are critically important, limiting girls' access to information and experiences can serve to backfire when they have to handle a difficult challenge. Parents often say, "We've talked about right and wrong, and my hope is that when she finds herself in that situation she will know what is right and what is wrong." This can certainly be true. Family values and norms can be deeply embedded in children and can serve as a moral compass that can help influence behavior. However, what can be equally powerful is for girls to actually have the experience of learning *how* to handle a situation and practice actually *doing so*.

We must balance our need to shelter and protect girls with the realization that they are eventually going to need to function in this world. While our tendency is to protect them and to want to handle challenges for them, we do girls a greater service by helping them develop the skills for themselves. This could mean helping them learn how to approach a teacher who may have scored their exam incorrectly, tell a dating partner that they do not want to go any further sexually, or refuse to ride in a car with someone who has been drinking. Letting girls know that these are dilemmas that they are likely to face and providing them the space to explore and practice their potential responses can increase a girl's sense of her ability to do the right thing in the actual situation.

A FUTURE FULL OF PROMISE

This book is not designed to illuminate all the things that are wrong in girls' lives. It has not been written to say "Look how bad everything is for girls." Conversely, the future for girls is bright. They have more opportunity than they've ever had to be successful, take risks, chart new paths, and live vast, varied, and fulfilling lives. They can play competitive and professional sports, go to college, medical school, law school, or graduate school. They can have unique and interesting careers, achieve business and political success, and give birth to and raise children and have a family. Girls are special, unique, and full of possibility. They have the opportunity to take a stand, set new records, and pave the way for an entire generation of girls who will follow.

The approach in this book is to look at the areas of a girl's life where she has the potential to be limited by her gender. What are the topics, concepts, and issues that can impact girls in negative or restrictive ways? We want girls to love being girls, but we also want them to have access to the broadest range of opportunities and possibilities. We want to prepare them for the rewards and challenges that they will face and we want to equip them with the skills that they will need to negotiate their growing up years.

Girls have all the potential in the world, but they need adults in their lives who will help guide them, protect them, nurture them, and challenge them. They need people who will have honest conversations with them and prepare them for the often difficult challenges that they will face. They need caring adults who recognize the pressures that they face, understand the realities of their lives, and work to ensure an equitable and just future for all girls. It is my hope that you also believe this, and this is why you are reading this book.

CHAPTER 2

Girly Girls

Pretty, Pink, Skinny, and Sexy

There is a lot of pressure for us to look a certain way. We are supposed to be pretty, and skinny, and have big boobs and nice hair. The pressure comes from our friends, from boys, and even from our parents. I know a girl whose mom buys her padded bras and high heels. They go to the salon and get fake nails and spray tans. We are only in sixth grade. . . . If I did that my mom would kill me!

—Leah, sixth grade

A shopping trip for a friend who recently had a baby girl resulted in a frustrated attempt to find an appropriate gift that was not pink. I do love the color pink; however, I knew that everyone was going to arrive with a pink gift, as seems to be the case for all new baby girls. As I perused the baby clothes, blankets, toys, and accessories, I was dazzled by all the tiny pink choices!

I wondered why, at such an early age, pink is seen as the only appropriate color for a baby girl? From the moment the announcement is made, "It's a girl!" we already have expectations on what the baby should wear and what colors are most appropriate for a little baby girl or boy. In general, I think we find comfort in the regularity of pink for girls and blue for boys. In fact, if a baby is not wearing one of the assigned colors, we may be initially unsure of the sex of the child. Have you ever seen a baby that was not dressed in pink or blue and felt confused as to what the sex of the baby was, what you should say to the parents, or how you should comment on the child?

Research studies have observed people's reactions toward babies who are wrapped in a pink blanket or a blue blanket. How would people respond to the baby based entirely on the color of the blanket? Would they do or say anything different if the baby was in pink or in blue?

When they saw a baby wrapped in a pink blanket, they over-whelmingly commented on the baby's delicate features and physical beauty. When the same baby was wrapped in a blue blanket, people commented about how strong or strapping the baby was. If the baby was wrapped in yellow or green, most people thought twice about what they should say. What is the appropriate reaction now? They didn't want to say or do anything wrong or make an incorrect guess as to the baby's sex.

EARLY EXPECTATIONS FOR BOYS AND GIRLS

From the time a baby is born, there are expectations in place that are based exclusively on the baby's physical sex. These expectations define feminine and masculine gender for girls and boys, women and men. Early in life, we begin to place value on certain traits or specific characteristics that we associate with boys or girls, and we may unconsciously impose rules or limits based on what is generally considered acceptable for either gender. How do these early impressions or expectations translate into our ongoing thoughts about what is right for boys and girls?

Carol Gilligan, a prominent Harvard psychologist who has studied the development of girls, believes that girls construct their identities and their understanding of their gender based on how other people respond to them (Gilligan, 1982). Girls develop thoughts, feelings, and behaviors based on the messages that they receive from others regarding what it means to be a girl. For example, children generally learn at very young ages that girls, but not boys, wear dresses. They also learn that girls play with dolls and boys play with trucks. Boys don't cry. Girls don't fight. Girls do the dishes, and boys take out the garbage. The interactions that we have with children can help shape their understanding of what it means to be a boy or girl and can influence what they perceive to be "appropriate behavior" for their gender.

Activity: Who Does What?

Consider the following common tasks, chores, and activities. As you read through the list, can you easily assign an "expected gender" to the task? Are there items that jump out in your mind as things that, in general, girls/women do and things that, in general, boys/men do?

- Takes out the garbage
- Goes golfing
- Cooks dinner
- Hosts a dinner party
- Cleans the house
- Drinks beer
- Cuts the grass
- Drinks wine
- Plants the flowers
- Buys new shoes
- Washes the car
- Plays video games
- Does the laundry
- Watches documentaries
- Organizes the carpool
- Reads fashion magazines

- Buys the groceries
- Reads sports magazines
- Irons the clothes
- Plays baseball
- Cleans the garage
- Tap dances
- Feeds the baby
- Goes to the PTA meetings
- Writes the thank-you notes
- Goes to the spa
- Bakes the birthday cakes
- Vacuums the carpet
- Pays the bills
- Changes the oil in the car
- Changes the diapers
- Drives on a date

As you completed the activity above, did you find that many of the tasks are stereotypically assigned to a specific gender? Some are a bit more obvious than others but, of course, *all* are activities that both men and women can, and do, engage in. Did you notice whether or not *you* participate in more of the gender typical or gender atypical activities? It can sometimes be difficult to step outside of the expected roles. Think about stay-at-home parents, for example. There would be nothing unusual for a mother to be a stay-at-home parent; it is much less frequent that a father is a stay-at-home parent.

As it can be difficult for adults to cross the lines of typical gender expectations, it can also be difficult for both boys and girls to do this as well. Girls worry that they will be judged or ridiculed in some way because they are different. Janya, a sixth grade girl said,

I think that everyone expects girls to play with dolls and makeup and do super-girly stuff. I like doing girly things sometimes, but I would rather play outside with my older brothers. I am really good at sports, but sometimes I feel like people tell me I should be quieter and act more 'like a lady.' I guess I am a tomboy.

Clearly, Janya is dealing with the pressure that she feels from others to be or act in a certain way. She knows what she likes and what she is good at but also recognizes that some of the things she enjoys do not necessarily fit with what she has learned girls are supposed to do or be.

While girls now have more options than ever before to explore their interests and skills, they still recognize that there are expectations that people put upon them based on their gender. I've talked to many parents, teachers, and counselors who say that they treat both boys and girls the same and tell them both that they can be and do anything that they want. They see increased equality surrounding the things that girls can do such as get good grades, play sports, and go to college. However, when I talk to girls, they say that they feel intense pressure around fitting in, looking good, and being pretty. The girls often feel more pressure around what they think they are *supposed to look like*, than they feel around what they think they are *supposed to do*.

WHAT DO YOU LIKE ABOUT BEING A GIRL?

The understanding of the term *femininity*, or the quality of being female, has changed over the years. Once thought of as nurturing, caretaking, and domestic, femininity now most often seems to be equated to fashion, beauty, and sex appeal. Over time, sociologists and psychologists have explored the concept of femininity and the feminine gender role. Most of the ways that femininity has been historically discussed and defined has been in relation to family and domestic skills, beauty and looks, and acquisition of male attention.

While many of us would like to believe that this definition has evolved, research shows that very little has actually changed as it relates to the expectations that society has for girls, and very little has changed about how girls internalize, or think and feel about, their own gender. While girls have more opportunities around sports, college, careers, and relationships, there are still rigid expectations to which girls and women are held that can, unfortunately, limit a girl's sense of herself and her abilities.

One of the questions that we have asked several hundred girls in our research is, "What do you like about being a girl?" Overwhelmingly, girls said things such as, "I can get my nails and hair done" and "We can wear skirts and frilly dresses" and "I can get my daddy to buy me things." A full 85 percent of the responses to this question fell into the categories of physical beauty, material possessions, and getting what you want. The remaining 15 percent of the responses included themes revolving around childbirth and mothering, emotions, friendships, and family.

Activity: Redefining Femininity

As recently as 20 years ago, Fiebert (1990) defined the feminine role as having four different dimensions:

1. Adherence to cultural fashion and beauty standards

2. Performance of family and domestic skills

3. Satisfaction of the needs of others

4. Acquisition of male attention

If we want girls to be feminine, does it mean that these are the things they should be working toward? Are there more empowering messages that we can give girls about what it means to be a girl and what femininity looks like? What do you think are some of the different ways that girls can conceptualize femininity?

1. _____

2. _____

3. _____

4. _____

Somehow, femininity—and being a girl—has been defined as external beauty, sexuality, and even manipulation. These are not inherent qualities that girls possess, nor are girls "hardwired" to love fashion and beauty. The way that we, as adults, shape girls' understanding of femininity can impact the way that they view being a girl, as well as the qualities they perceive as appropriately feminine. We want girls to connect with femininity as a concept that is not exclusively connected to beauty, male attention, or domestic pursuits. While these may be important facets of a girl's life, these components do not have to be the only way that feminine is defined. When we equate femininity, or being a girl, to these limited concepts, we restrict girls' options, their creativity, and their sense of themselves as complex, smart, and valuable. We must redefine for girls what feminine can actually mean.

FEMININE = PRETTY = SKINNY

Part of how girls understand femininity is, of course, looking feminine. Girls have shared at length the pressures they feel to look a certain way, have specific styles or brands of clothes, and possess ideal body characteristics. Girls also go to great lengths to achieve a specific look. Skin, hair, nails, eyebrows, breasts, legs, eyelashes, lips, stomach, eyes, nose, butt, and teeth are all body parts that girls report wanting to change. They go to tanning salons, straighten their hair, get colored contacts, whiten their teeth, wax their eyebrows, pad their bras, and starve their bodies in an attempt to achieve what they see as ideal beauty. We can clearly see in the media that girls are exposed to images of women that are overtly sexual, very thin, and with unrealistic and surgically enhanced proportions. In turn, one of the biggest struggles that girls experience is pressure to look a certain way. This "certain way" varies somewhat based on environment, culture, and ethnicity, but overwhelmingly girls report experiencing the pressures of the mainstream media on a daily basis. Many know what it feels like to spend hours of time each day thinking about their appearance, their body size and shape, and what they will wear.

We know that early exposure to some of these beauty ideas can be harmful to girls. Girls who are exposed to media images that promote a thin-as-ideal body actually have increased dissatisfaction with their own body. The longer they are exposed to these kinds of images or messages, the more dissatisfied they become and the more likely they are to report being on a diet. This was found to be the case even among girls who were already thin with low body mass indexes as well as with very young girls (Knobloch-Westerwick & Crane, 2012).

Activity: Helping Girls Critically Analyze the Media

The images of women in magazines, on commercials, and throughout the media are often overtly sexual, airbrushed, cropped, and resized. The skin of black women is often lightened in print media and complexions of models are edited to look as though they have no pores and flawless skin. Even famous supermodels do not look the same in real life as they do in magazines. Girls often see these images and feel that this skinny, pretty, sexy ideal is what they should look like and is the image that they should emulate. We want girls to recognize that these images are not actually real; rather, they are edited and refined to look flawless. We want girls to develop a critical eye when it comes to media consumption and possess the ability to recognize the difference between a "real" body and a computer-generated body and to be cautious of judging their own bodies against these unrealistic images.

Have girls peruse a variety of magazines: teen, men's, cooking, sports, entertainment, and so forth. Have them identify the healthy and the unhealthy bodies in each magazine. Encourage them to critically analyze what the photos represent and how they portray girls and women. Can they find images of women with healthy and realistic bodies as well as discern the bodies that are manipulated, computer generated, or airbrushed? Do they notice the way that women's sexuality is often used in advertising?

While these popular media and cultural images can play a significant role in how we feel about ourselves and our bodies, the messages that we receive from parents, teachers, and peers are also critically important. I saw this first hand with Meghan, a young woman who struggles with issues around body image. She shared with me that at least half of the thoughts that she has on a daily basis revolve around her weight, her eating, and her appearance. She, at age 21, says that she feels better and more confident when she is thinner and that she will avoid going places or meeting up with friends if she feels like she has gained weight or does not look "presentable."

I was interested in learning when her thoughts and negative feelings about her body began. She told me that when she was in second grade she went on her first diet. Her mother was on Weight Watchers, as were all her mother's friends. She said she remembers them all being over for lunch one day and all they talked about was food, diets, exercise, and fitting into a bikini in the summer. Meghan said that day she went to her room and looked at her own body in the mirror. She said she never wore a bikini before and thought that she needed to be slimmer to do that. She began to notice that she was not as small as the other girls in her grade and made the decision to start a diet. She said ever since second grade she has been on some type of diet or eating plan and was constantly trying to lose weight. Over ten years later, and well within a healthy weight range, Meghan is still dealing with feelings of inadequacy, low self-esteem, and negative body image. She says,

I also remember when I was in elementary school, my dad came up to me and kind of pinched my stomach and made a comment about my weight. I don't really think he was trying to be mean, but that experience has stuck with me for all of these years. I can still feel the exact feelings that I felt on that day when that happened. My dad is my best friend but also my biggest critic. When I slip up with my eating, he is the first person who will comment on it.

As we can see from Meghan's situation, our issues with food and eating do not disappear when we become adults. Many of the insecurities and pressures that we had as young girls continue for us well into our adulthood. When I talk to parents and teachers about some of these issues, I always bring up the infamous office potluck. Lots of schools and offices have potluck lunches or birthday lunches where everyone is responsible for bringing something to contribute. Rarely can we observe an entire lunch without hearing multiple comments about diet, weight, what we can or should eat, and what is off-limits. "Oh, those brownies look so delicious, but I just shouldn't" or "I am cheating today and going to have to do some extra time at the gym tomorrow" or "As soon as this diet is over I can't wait to eat some pizza!"

Regardless of the actual comments, it is rare that you can have a room of women together with food without there being negative and self-deprecating dialogue.

Activity: Observe the Potluck and the Dieters

Many of us will be at lunch or dinner at some point in the future with a group of friends or colleagues. Pay attention to who in the group is more likely to talk about food, calories, diets, fat, exercise, or guilt. Do more men or women obsess about their eating? Who is on a diet in the group and how do you know that?

While girls are watching these subtle, or more indirect, comments that we make around food, eating, body size and shape, they are also profoundly impacted by our more direct comments and behaviors. Girls all around us are paying attention to our own relationship with food. They watch what we eat, how we talk about food, and how we talk about our own bodies. The role that we, as adults, have in shaping girls' attitudes about their own bodies cannot be overstated. We can see from Meghan's story that her early interactions with her mother and father around her body and eating have stuck with her as an adult and significantly impact how she thinks about herself today.

The comments that Meghan experienced and observed were obviously damaging, but they were even less overt and direct than some girls experience from their parents. One parent, proudly shared a story about how she was dealing with Zoe, her "chubby 6-year-old daughter." The mother, a middle school vice principal in an affluent suburb, was complaining about her daughter's overeating and recent weight gain. She shared that on a recent shopping trip to the mall she planned to "nip that problem in the bud." The mother stated that, "I marched Zoe right down to the Lane Bryant store and told her that if she keeps it up, this will be the only store where she would be able to buy clothes."

In the same way that Meghan clearly remembers what it felt like when her father pinched her stomach, I imagine 6-year-old Zoe will have a similar, destructive memory of her experience. It is hard to believe that an adult would proudly share this story, but it reiterates the fact that just because we grow up and become adults does not mean we figure out how to address complicated issues and internal insecurities. Zoe will face pressures around her looks and body size from the media and from society and will also have to endure the negative pressures and feedback from her mother. Unfortunately, she is a girl who will be a prime candidate for developing an eating disorder when she hits her teenage years.

As we think about redefining femininity to be healthier and less limiting for girls, perhaps one of the first components should be to encourage girls to have a strong and healthy body rather than a skinny body.

HOW I THINK I LOOK = HOW I FEEL ABOUT MYSELF

One of the most important predictors of self-esteem in girls is their own thoughts about their appearance and body weight. Girls' perception of their appearance impacts their self-esteem more than girls' self-esteem impacts their perception of their appearance. That means that the way girls think they look has more to do with how they feel about themselves than almost anything else. Young women report that their body weight is the aspect of their life with which they are most dissatisfied (Kutob, Senf, Crago, & Shisslak, 2010).

This seems to be the case for Meghan, discussed above, who told me that she estimates that about 80 percent of how she feels about herself is related to how she feels about her body and if she feels skinny or pretty. She said the other 20 percent is connected to her other characteristics such as who she is as a friend, if she is kind, and her relationships with her family.

If the number one thing that influences and impacts girls' self-esteem is the perceptions that they hold of their bodies and the thoughts they have about their own physical attractiveness, then girls are viewing their appearance as their major sense of worth. When physical beauty and external traits and characteristics are constantly reinforced as important for girls at the expense of other traits, skills, and characteristics, we are—perhaps subconsciously—telling girls that their value comes largely from their outward appearance.

Is this too far fetched? Probably not. In our research with girls, we have seen that they place extreme emphasis on outward appearance and especially on being sexy and attractive to boys. Girls talk about the importance of being "tall and skinny, with big boobs and nice hair," and why wouldn't they? This is the consistent image that they receive from the mainstream media on what is attractive, beautiful, feminine, and sexy.

With body image so tightly connected to self-esteem, how can we change the way that girls feel about and experience their own bodies? We have to find ways to impact the messages that girls receive surrounding body image and ideal bodies. This is not accomplished by simply telling girls that all body shapes and sizes are beautiful. We must make concentrated efforts to assist girls in learning how to base their self-esteem on personal attributes other than body weight and shape.

Girls have so many positive qualities that are not associated with looks; however, these qualities are rarely emphasized. In much the same way that the baby in the pink blanket receives comments and compliments about being pretty or delicate, adolescent girls also receive many more compliments about their appearance than they do about their other qualities or their abilities. We need to help girls focus on their positive qualities, traits, and characteristics that are not related to body image. When girls are able to do this, their perceptions of their body shape change and they experience less body dissatisfaction. Girls who can identify the things that they do well and the positive characteristics that they possess tend to rely less on weight and body shape to determine their self-esteem (Armitage, 2012). Simply stated, when girls recognize that they are good at things other than being pretty, they experience higher levels of self-esteem.

Activity: Strength Bombardment

Sometimes it is difficult for girls to identify their positive traits. Having a group of girls participate in an activity called a strength bombardment gives girls the opportunity to identify the traits and characteristics of their peers that they admire and allows girls to hear positive comments from an entire group of girls.

This activity can be used with a group of girls who already know each other. The group sits in a circle and one person at a time takes a turn sitting in the middle of the circle. The person who is in the middle should not speak; rather, she should just listen to the comments made by each person in the circle. Each person in the circle takes a turn sharing a positive comment or compliment about the person who is in the middle of the circle . . . but the comment cannot be related to looks, beauty, clothes, or any external factor. Compliments and comments must be related to character, kindness, behavior, and work ethic—internal qualities.

After each girl in the circle shares a comment about the girl in the middle, the girl in the middle should say thank you and return to her seat in the circle. The next group member then can make her way to the center of the circle and the process is repeated until all girls have participated.

FEMININE = PRETTY = SKINNY = SEXY

Girls in elementary school begin to understand at a very young age concepts around beauty, desire, and sexual appeal. In talking to a group of fifth grade girls about what they think are some of the big issues going on for girls their age, several girls talked about "looking nice for boys" and "boys wanting to kiss you and touch you." As girls get older, the intensity of their responses increases. But the theme is consistent—being feminine means being pretty, skinny . . . and sexy. Girls report pressure to be sexy and to receive attention from boys and to compete with other girls for boys' attention.

I feel like girls are in constant competition with each other. We want to be smarter than other girls, prettier than other girls, skinnier than other girls, and sexier than other girls. We want boys to pay more attention to us than to the others. There is a girl at my school who gets up at 5:00 in the morning and literally spends like two hours getting ready for school every morning. She always looks perfect and, in gym class, I don't even think that she sweats. She has big boobs and she wears tight shirts and the guys, like, follow her around the school; it is so annoying. —Lora, tenth grade

The pressure for girls to be sexy can begin for girls as early as elementary school. A recent study found that girls as young as 6 years old want to look and dress sexy and that they equate sexiness with popularity (Starr & Ferguson, 2012). By fourth and fifth grade, girls are dressing more adult-like and wearing clothing that is sexually revealing or suggestive. Padded bras and thong underwear can be bought for elementary school-aged girls, and low-rider jeans, yoga pants, and low-cut tops are the dress of choice for many teen girls today. Even among school spirit and athletic wear, the trend toward sexier clothes is evident.

Case Study: It's Just Fashion, or Is It?

School Spirit Wear

As I have talked to many school staff, coaches, and administrators about the issue of sexualization of girls, invariably, a question of school spirit gear and athletic uniforms arises. The following are two recent examples that illustrate this point.

Lots of schools have school stores where you can purchase school sweatshirts, hats, and "spirit wear." Additionally, many girls' athletic teams have shorts, warm-up suits, or sweat suits that they wear on game day or prior to a sporting event. One recent trend has been for the school mascot name to be printed on the backside of the shorts or pants. We must ask the question, Why would we, as adults who are selecting and designing the spirit wear, want to draw attention to the backsides of our elementary, middle, and high school girls? Are we saying this increases school spirit? The girls wearing the shorts can't even see the printing on the back; rather, the design is exclusively for the benefit of the observer.

With an increased understanding of this issue, one school program opted to stop printing yoga pants for girls with the program name on the backside; rather, it began placing the printing down the front of the leg.

(Continued)

(Continued)

The girls at the school went crazy! They scrounged through the old boxes trying to find the last few pairs of pants that still had the printing on the backside. They wanted to fit in and be fashionable—they probably didn't see themselves as being sexualized.

Athletic Uniforms

A second, recent example was with a junior varsity girls' volleyball team. Athletic uniforms have evolved over the years and, in some cases, not for the better. The modern trend for the volleyball short is the tinier, the better. Among girls as young as elementary school, shorts are skin tight and often so short that the lower cheeks of the buttocks can be seen. Teachers report that high school girls actually hitch up their shorts to the point they actually look more like cheeky underwear or a bathing suit bottom, than an athletic uniform. While we must recognize that all sports have uniforms designed to enhance play and performance, it is hard to understand how these tiny bottoms help a young girl perform better at this sport.

One junior varsity volleyball coach sought to impose a more modest short for his team. While still a modern, spandex-style, very short bottom, the new uniform short was just a bit less revealing than what other teams were wearing. Thinking that parents would be grateful for this change, you can imagine his surprise when it was the mothers of the players that began calling him to complain about the uniforms and insist on a smaller, shorter bottom!

Girls learn very early that they are sexual beings. They are taught that their value comes from being pretty and sexy, and they learn through socialization and their interactions with others that receiving sexual attention is important. Patrice Oppliger (2008) suggests that young women are pushed toward external validation and objectification based on the insecurities that are brought on by ongoing exposure to media images of "perfect" women. It should come as no surprise then, when girls begin to embody what has been reinforced for them for many years—be pretty and sexy. Adolescent girls begin acting out sexually, seeking sexual attention, and connecting their own value to the ways that others respond to them or give them attention.

I think there is a lot of pressure for us to look a certain way. Like if you don't have certain brands of clothes or if you don't have big boobs, people are going to make fun of you. I think we want to look nice for ourselves, but we also want boys to pay attention to us. And we know what they like too. —Tina, seventh grade

Girls recognize that their bodies can get attention from boys and men, and they learn at early ages how to get this attention. Unfortunately, we, as adults, have a great deal of responsibility for how girls understand their own sexuality and their bodies as sexual objects. A 2010 American Psychological Association report entitled "The Sexualization of Girls," examines a concept called *sexualization*. It discusses the ways that girls become sexualized—or valued for their sexuality or sex appeal over all other traits and characteristics—at very young ages. When physical attractiveness is equated to being sexy and a person is sexually objectified—or treated as if they have been made for someone else's sexual use—a person has been sexualized. For girls, this is happening at younger and younger ages as girls learn to equate value with being pretty and being pretty with being sexy. Girls learn to objectify themselves by what we teach them . . . and then we judge them.

> *I really don't understand why girls dress like they do. It's almost like they are asking guys for attention with their low-cut tops, jeans with their underwear hanging out of the back, and a ton of makeup. I mean what do they really expect a guy to think, that they don't want his attention? They are trying so hard to make themselves look older than they are, and they end up looking cheap and easy.*
> —High School Teacher

MY BODY IS FOR OTHER PEOPLE

Should we blame girls for how they are dressing and for adopting the messages that have been reinforced for them on what it means to be a girl, what it means to be feminine, and what is valuable and important? What are the messages that are internalized for a young girl when her value is connected to, and judged almost exclusively on, how she looks? When a girl sexualizes herself, objectifies her own body, and harshly judges her own appearance, we see the internalization of all the messages that she has received about her value (APA, 2010). *Body objectification* is when we believe that our body exists for the benefit of another person's gaze and desire (Tolman, Impett, Tracy, & Michael, 2006).

When we emphasize the sexuality of young girls and encourage their receipt of sexual attention, we are objectifying them and we are teaching them to objectify themselves. When girls are sexualized, they can experience negative effects in a variety of areas, including (APA, 2010)

- cognitive functioning—difficulty concentrating and completing mental activities.
- emotional functioning—lowered confidence and increased levels of shame, anxiety, and self-disgust.
- mental health—increased prevalence of eating disorders, low self-esteem, and depression.
- sexuality—diminished sexual health and sexual assertiveness.

These issues are intense and long lasting. Girls' early experiences have a significant role in how they come to understand themselves and value themselves. If they are not getting the attention or the approval they have learned to seek, they believe themselves to be not good enough. Thus, we reinforce the ideas that value comes from femininity, looks, body size, and sex appeal.

We need to help girls develop a healthy image of their bodies, a sense that their bodies are not designed for the pleasure of others, and the understanding that their sense of worth and value does not come from others finding them pretty or sexy.

WHAT CAN WE DO?

☆ Encourage girls to identify their strengths and talents

We are all good at different things, but sometimes it is difficult to truly identify what those things actually are. Girls have a very difficult time believing that they are good at many things. In fact, research from the American Association of University Women (1995) found, by high school, only 27 percent of girls would report that they are good at a lot of things. This is down from 47 percent in elementary school. When I am working with girls in individual counseling, I often ask them to tell me what they do well. More often than not, this ends up being a homework assignment for them because they can't come up with a list on the spot. We need to help girls find their value through their skills, talents, and interests.

☆ Teach life skills to girls

Life skills are not skills for boys or skills for girls. Girls need to know how to change a tire, shovel snow, stand up for themselves, jump rope, play chess, throw a baseball, and cut the grass. These are not activities that either boys or girls can inherently do better, but they are skills that we tend to see become assigned to one gender or the other. Girls and boys need to develop skills in all areas.

☆ Emphasize and compliment internal rather than external traits

As a society, we easily notice and compliment the external characteristics of others. How often do we hear, "You look great, have you lost weight?" or "You're hair looks great!" or "I love that outfit" and "You must have been in the sun, your skin is glowing." It is much easier to comment on these factors; however, in doing so we reinforce the value placed on external factors and/or looks. The following chart provides examples of external versus internal traits.

External	*Internal*
Body Shape	Competence
Weight/Body Size	Persistence
Clothes	Courage
Hair	Performance
Skin Tone	Character

☆ Pay attention to the way that you talk about your own body and about food

Girls who have mothers who diet and constantly talk about food, calories, and body size are far more likely to develop issues around their own bodies at very early ages. Additionally, pay attention to what you say about food and calorie consumption in front of girls. Girls are watching us when we comment on how everything looks so delicious, but we "shouldn't," "couldn't," or "mustn't" have dessert. Pay attention next time at that office meal or potluck and see how many people comment on their food selections. Also, notice if your visceral reaction is to participate in this dialogue as well.

☆ Host a "No-Fat Talk" Day/Week/Month

This is an opportunity to point out the ways in which our ongoing discussions and thoughts are pervasively centered on how fat we are. Several groups, including the Eating Concerns Advisors and the national sorority Tri Delta, have sponsored and publicized events focused on limiting the negative messages we give ourselves about our bodies. An undertaking such as this actually is a harder concept to pull off than you might think. Try it with a friend first and see how often you talk about weight, body shape, eating, calories, and so on in a specific period of time.

☆ Emphasize strong, healthy bodies rather than thin bodies

Skinny does not necessarily equal healthy. The media has a focus on lean body shapes for women and 95 percent of fashion models are lean. In women's fitness magazines, 55 percent of the models are lean and 36 percent are muscular. Only 6 percent of the images of women in either type of magazine had a softer or more curvaceous body type (Wasulkiw, Emms, Meuse, & Poirier, 2009). When you see billboards, advertisements, magazines, music videos, and television commercials, ask girls to identify the bodies that look strong and healthy. What do they notice about the differences between the various body types? What is realistic and attainable, and what type of body requires starving oneself or having plastic surgery?

☆ Point out to girls unrealistic images of girls and women in the media, on television, and in magazines

In most cases the advertisements and photographs of women that are featured in print media consist of images that have been computer enhanced, photoshopped, and airbrushed. The result is a final product that is actually no longer a real person.

The Renfrew Center, an eating disorders treatment facility, has a campaign with stickers that you can purchase and place on magazines and print media that are in your home or office (http:// renfrewcenter.com/resources/action-resource-guides). The stickers are shaped like caution signs and say, "This promotes eating disorders" or "This promotes healthy body image." Provide girls an opportunity to explore media and magazines and identify for themselves what a healthy body actually looks like versus a fake body versus an unhealthy body. Having an ability to critically analyze the media is of paramount importance in the development of a healthy sense of self.

☆ Pay attention to how you think about and reinforce traditional expectations around masculinity and femininity

Do you have long-standing beliefs about what boys and girls are supposed to do or supposed to be good at? Do girls who do not fit into a traditional mold get treated differently? When we reinforce the traditional ideals for girls, we limit them and their options. We must encourage strength, determination, and competence in girls. Teachers can ensure that room tasks are evenly divided between girls and boys and that every time there is a physical task to be completed a boy is not automatically chosen for the job. Similarly, boys can be selected for domestic or caretaking room tasks demonstrating that the chores are not inherently masculine or feminine.

☆ Recognize that girls feel pressure to dress in the ways that they see others dressing

Merely forbidding girls to wear certain clothes does not do anything to create awareness or an understanding of themselves as sexual objects. Setting rules about what should or should not be worn can serve to backfire and reinforce the idea that we—the adults—have absolutely no idea of the difficulty of the teen's life and the social pressures that she is experiencing. Talk to girls about the societal pressures surrounding looks and sexuality. Allow them to explore the feelings that they have and the messages that they receive in a place that is safe and nonjudgmental.

CHAPTER 3

Drama! Mean Girls and Real Housewives

I don't even understand how it happened. We were all best friends one day, and then it seemed like overnight everything changed. I don't even know what I did. But somehow, my friend—I guess I should call her my ex-friend—got it in her mind that I was talking to her boyfriend or something and then the next day at school the entire group ignored me. They conveniently didn't have an extra seat for me at the lunch table, and then at volleyball practice they would not even make eye contact with me. When I walked into the locker room, everyone just stopped talking and stared at me. Then that same night, on Facebook, they were posting all of these messages about how "true friends don't steal each other's boyfriends" and "that it is good to know who in life you can really trust and who you can't" and "be careful, you can be surprised when you learn that the people who you thought were your friends are really backstabbing whores"—yes, they called me a backstabbing whore and I didn't even do anything! I can't even figure out where this all came from, who started it, or how to make it stop. It just feels like it is out of control and there is nothing I can do. I hate all of this drama!

—Morgan, eleventh grade

GIRL DRAMA

Every time I speak to a group of girls, teachers, counselors, or parents about what they think are the big things going on for girls, without a doubt the first issue that comes out of everyone's mouth is drama! When I ask girls what they mean by *drama*, girls say, "You know—he said, she said stuff" and "girls trying to take your boyfriend" or "girls who are spreading rumors and lies about you."

Drama is the word that girls use to describe the frustrations of their social lives, the difficulties that they have navigating relationships, and the challenges they face communicating effectively with their friends.

Teachers and counselors describe drama a little differently. They say, "It's girls excluding each other from parties and social events," and "girls fighting over boyfriends or making fun of other girls' clothes," and "girls just being downright mean to one another; I don't get it why these girls are so cruel," and finally, "I think it is just girls being girls."

As girls get to late elementary school, issues with friendships and relationships with other girls have increased importance, and by middle school nearly 80 percent of girls say that friendship and girl drama is a big issue facing girls their age. Often the aggressive behavior that happens between girls is overlooked as simply, "Girls being girls." There is often the expectation that girls are "catty," "will stab you in the back," and lack authenticity in relationships. As Tiana, a seventh grade girl stated, "I think people expect girls to compete with each other. They like to see a cat fight."

Adults question, "Why are these girls so mean? Why don't they care about anyone else's feelings? When do they grow out of this horrible stage? Is this aggression and meanness just part of girlhood?"

While these are all legitimate questions, the real question that we want to answer is, "What is going on in the lives of girls that makes their social aggression so pervasive? And is there anything that we can do to change it?"

Boys and girls both go through a period of time when they navigate and negotiate friendships and relationships, but there seem to be big differences in how they approach these processes and how they approach conflict. Girls tend to have more difficulty than boys do in directly addressing conflict and they tend to use different strategies when managing tumultuous situations or relationships. As one teacher said, "Guys will get in a fight one day and then be cool with each other the next day. Girls hang on to this stuff for years. It is almost like they enjoy the drama."

WHAT IS RELATIONAL AGGRESSION?

Relational aggression is girl bullying. It is the way in which girls use their relationships with one another to be mean, manipulative, exclusionary, and hostile (Grotpeter & Crick, 1996). While bullying in schools has received much attention in recent years and many schools and concerned communities are doing more to address this important topic, few have figured out how to address the more covert bullying that often takes place between and among girls. Many states have adopted legislation that requires schools to develop and implement policies that address bullying and cyberbullying, and some of girls' relationally aggressive behavior falls into these categories. However, the more covert forms of bullying that are most common between and among girls—relational bullying and aggression—can be overlooked because they rarely include physical acts of intimidation (Young, Boye, & Nelson, 2006). When aggression is relational, it does not necessarily assume the power differential as defined in traditional bullying—picture the big kid stealing the smaller kid's lunch money. Relational aggression is a type of aggression that occurs through the relationships that we have with one another. Individuals who use relational aggression often know one another, have (or have had) close friendships or relationships with one another, and may be in the same social circles.

Relational aggression includes "sarcastic verbal comments, speaking to another in a cold or hostile tone of voice, ignoring, staring, gossiping, spreading rumors, 'mean' facial expressions, and exclusion, all acts aimed to damage the target's social status or self-esteem" (Remillard & Lamb, 2005, p. 221). In other words, relationally aggressive relationships are based on intimacy, and they use the relationship as a tool to manipulate. Overtly aggressive relationships are based on a desire to act aggressively, intimidate, or control another person. Relational aggression is much less obvious but can often be much more damaging.

Recently, there has been an increase in information available on relational aggression through popular media such as movies, books, television shows, and websites. We have seen it portrayed in the movies, such as "Mean Girls," as upper class girls who exclude one another from social circles and events. Rachel Simmons' book, *Odd Girl Out* (2002), discusses the hidden culture of aggression in girls. There has also been a great deal of academic research by scholars such as Crick and Grotpeter (2005) and Remillard and Lamb (2005), that has contributed to our intellectual understanding of what relational aggression actually looks like among girls.

Girls use acquaintances, friendships, and even dating relationships as fodder for aggression in a different way than boys do. Though both boys and girls can be aggressive, we tend to see more overt and physical aggression in boys and more relational and manipulative aggression exhibited by girls. When I met Sadie, a tenth grader, and heard her story, I became increasingly aware that relational aggression is intense and can truly impact any girl regardless of her ethnicity, social status, income, or intelligence level. Sadie lives in an affluent community, with both of her caring and involved parents. She is an honor roll student, an athlete, and has been generally well liked by her peers. She has an older sister and a younger brother. She is attractive, intelligent, and very social.

I'm in the school musical and am totally consumed with that right now so I haven't been hanging out with my 'usual group' of friends as much as I normally do. There is this group of girls and we have been friends for the entire year. We hang out after school and on the weekends together—I thought everything was cool. Then one of the guys that one of my friends liked started talking to me. I thought he was really cute, and they weren't dating or anything, so I didn't think it was a big deal if I just talked to him. We hung out one time at the varsity basketball game and apparently it was a really big deal to my 'so-called' friends. Before I even got to school the next day, there were Facebook postings, tweets, and texts going around saying stuff like, "Sadie is a dirty slut" and "Watch out or Sadie will have sex with your boyfriend" and "Sadie does 'such-and-so' to boys in the bathroom," and there were even worse ones if you can believe that. It was like in a matter of hours the entire school was talking about me and none of it was true! It's been a couple of months and nothing has been the same. I mean, all

*you can really do is tell people that the rumors aren't true, but once
people get something in their mind it is really hard to change it.
I can't stand school right now. . . I mean I really hate going there.*

Unfortunately, Sadie's experience is not at all unique. Girls,
parents, and teachers give similar examples of how they see girls
gossip, spread rumors, and be mean to one another in very intense
and intentional ways. With the proliferation of technology and
the use of social media as primary tools of communication, bullying and relational aggression can now take place at any moment
of the day or night—not merely during the school hours. Students
who once were able to retreat from a hostile school environment
during the evenings or weekend are now susceptible to victimization 24 hours a day, 7 days a week. As one teacher said to me, "We
spend all day Monday dealing with what happened on Facebook
over the weekend. We essentially lose a day of learning."

I H8 U: GIRLS AND CYBERBULLYING

Technology has added a new dimension to girls' lives. While there
are tremendous benefits to the technological advances that we have
achieved, there is a very dark and dangerous side to technology as
well. The ability to monitor, stalk, spread rumors, and defame others has become easier and more anonymous through the use of the
internet. *Cyberbullying*, or the "willful and repeated harm inflicted
through the use of computers, cell phones, and other electronic
devices" (Patchin & Hinduja, 2012), has risen among teens over the
past several years and is a prevalent form of relational aggression
among girls. With the majority of U.S. teens having access to the
internet and to cell phones, the use of technology to bully others has
reached new heights. Teens have developed a preference for technology over face-to-face communication and interaction (D'Antona,
Kevorkian, & Russom, 2010) and over 82 percent of teens have
reported that someone else has said something mean or hurtful
about them online. What was once a post on the bathroom wall
where a handful of others could see has become a post on a Facebook
wall that hundreds or potentially thousands of "friends" can see.

Cyberbullying includes sending vicious or embarrassing text
messages, spreading rumors via cell phones or social networking,

creating web pages, videos, or profiles of another person on a social networking site to make fun of them and taking photos or videos and distributing them online (Patchin & Hinduja, 2012). This type of indirect aggression is consistent with the ways that girls bully one another, and the instantaneous nature of virtual communication means that rumors, gossip, pictures, and videos can go "viral" in a matter of seconds. An embarrassing moment caught on film is now shared with the entire school almost as quickly as it happens.

Cyberbullying differs from traditional bullying in that the victim may not know who the bully is or why they have been targeted. The virtual exchange also limits the ability to read visual cues and see the immediate impact of the communication. When we can't see the other person's reaction, we may fail to realize the depth to which our comments or actions may have hurt them. Girls will say and do things online that they would not say or do face-to-face. They can be cruel, sarcastic, and ruthless. Girls can take on different personas, manipulate their environments, and ostracize their peers. Girls who have experienced cyberbullying are less likely to enjoy school or feel safe at school. They have higher levels of depression, sadness, and anger and lower levels of self-esteem than their peers (D'Antona et al., 2010).

The following details some of the signs to look for if you suspect a teen is a victim or participant in cyberbullying behaviors:

Cyberbullying: What to Look For

Victims:	Bullies:
• Stops using their computer or cell phone	• Switches screens or closes programs on the computer when others walk by
• Becomes nervous or jumpy when getting an e-mail, text, Facebook notification	• Gets unusually upset if computer or cell phone privileges are restricted
• Experiences anxiety about going to school	• Avoids discussion about their computer or phone use
• Feels angry, depressed, frustrated after using the computer or cell phone	• Has more than one account or screen name
• Avoids discussion about their computer or phone use	*Source*: Merrell, Buchanan, & Tran (2006).

IS THIS JUST GIRLS BEING GIRLS?

It is probably safe to say that most people have engaged in some of the relationally aggressive behaviors discussed. Gossiping or ignoring somebody are probably things many of us have done at one time or another. But we must look at what point the behavior is normal and developmental and when the behavior is damaging and used to manipulate or ruin someone else's reputation.

The research that I conducted with girls revealed a difference between their definition of bullying behavior and their perception of their own experience in girl bullying. Specifically, girls were first asked if they had ever participated in girl bullying. In the survey, a little over 35 percent of the girls reported that they have engaged in girl bullying. Next, the girls were asked to respond to a series of behaviors and indicate whether or not they had participated in specific behaviors that we consider examples of girl bullying or relational aggression (i.e., teasing, excluding someone, spreading a rumor, lying about another girl, etc.). The results were markedly different. Over 70 percent of the girls reported engaging in teasing or name-calling, 53 percent stated that they had excluded someone from a social event. This tells us that the prevalence of actual relational aggression is extensive; however, girls do not define their own behavior as girl bullying.

It seems that the traditional definition of bullying, which is often perceived as physical aggression, such as pushing and shoving, does not necessarily resonate with girls. When they think of bullying, they are thinking of being pushed in the hall or someone stealing their lunch money. Girls are not necessarily defining the more subtle and relational bullying behaviors as actual bullying. So when they are engaging in more relational types of aggression, they do not see these behaviors as participation in bullying.

This became extremely evident to me as I was working with a group of eighth grade girls at an urban charter school. I had been asked to come to the school to work with a group of twelve girls who were deemed to be the problematic girls—the Queen Bees: the socialites, the bullies, the manipulators, and in some cases, the leaders. These were the girls who were creating the most distress for the entire grade, and perhaps the entire school.

When I got to the school and met the girls, I realized that the Queen Bees are not always the Queen Bees when they are in a group of all Queen Bees! At different times, in different environments, and around different groups of people, we tend to experience one another and ourselves differently. In some cases where we have more power, social capital, or privilege, we can use or exploit that differently than if we are in a situation where we perceive ourselves to have less power or authority. This also applies to girls in situations where they are with new or different groups of girls. There is a period of time where they seek to establish their social order or hierarchy. I watched as the girls negotiated their roles, attempted to exert their control over the group, and tried to determine who belonged where.

As we moved through the activities for the day and engaged the girls in a variety of activities related to building trust, increasing communication, and having a positive impact on the school climate, I quickly realized that these girls had very little awareness that they were, in fact, part of the problem. They actually went as far as to say that there is "no bullying that really happens at

Activity: Identifying Bullying and Relational Aggression

Help girls identify girl bullying behaviors and how their actions may be bullying and/or relational aggression. Individually or in small groups, have girls consider the following:
Do I:

- gossip or spread rumors about other girls?

- post things on Facebook or Twitter or other social media that could be embarrassing to another girl?

- ignore certain girls on purpose or intentionally exclude girls from "my group"?

- make fun of the clothes, appearance, or financial status of another girl?

- tell my friends who they can or should be friends with?

Take the time to explore with girls how and why they engage in any of these behaviors and help them strategize healthier ways to manage their anger and express their opinions. Also, discuss what girls can do when they observe other girls participating in girl bullying.

our school." When I asked what they meant by that the girls said, "Well, I mean, sometimes people will shove you in the hall or try to fight. But, in general, I don't think that we have a lot of bullying happening at our school."

I next asked the girls about the way that girls treat one another. I asked them if they see girls who spread rumors, exclude other girls from activities, and gossip about other girls in the school. At this point, they laughed and said that this sort of behavior happens all the time at their school! But that this was just how girls were, it wasn't really girls being bullies . . . just girls being girls. I wondered at what point social exclusion and rumor and gossip spreading had become a part of girls just being girls?

WHY ARE GIRLS SO MEAN TO EACH OTHER?

Researchers have attempted to understand why girls engage in relational forms of aggression more than physical forms of aggression and why girls seem to prefer engaging in more covert ways of harming their peers than boys do. Interesting research (Brown, 1998) has looked at gender role adherence and the way in which girls participate in and experience relational aggression. Specifically, researchers found that girls who follow along with more of the traditional stereotypical female behaviors are also more likely to engage in more relationally aggressive behavior. This is not to say that girls who merely look or act feminine are more relationally aggressive but rather the girls (and women) who buy into the ideas that girls are "supposed" to be or act certain conventional or stereotypical ways tend to engage in these more covert forms of bullying, social isolation, and peer exclusion than their peers who hold less stereotypical or traditional beliefs about how girls should act.

For many girls and women, embodying the female role means, in part, engaging in competition with other girls and women, criticizing and demeaning others' looks, behaviors, and thoughts, and isolating oneself from other girls while seeking the attention of men and boys. Relational aggression is a covert way of expressing anger, being dominant, and resolving conflict and tends to be more consistent with the social expectations placed on girls.

This makes sense because, in general, girls have been socialized to be kind and nice and to not be physically aggressive (Simmons,

Activity: Who is more likely to . . .

Think about the ways that boys and girls, or men and women, handle conflict. Who is more likely to:

- get into a physical fight at a bar?

- rally a group of friends to ignore or exclude someone?

- punch a wall in frustration?

- spread a nasty rumor?

- be nice to someone's face and then talk about them behind their back?

- be on the same sports team and get into a physical fight during practice?

2009). While boys and girls both get angry at similar rates, they learn to manage their anger differently (Brown, 1998). Girls are taught from very young ages that aggression and fighting physically is not particularly acceptable or permissible for girls. Girls who get in physical fights often receive bad reputations and have lower acceptance from peers than boys who physically fight with their peers. While there are certainly very physically aggressive girls and girls who pride themselves on their physical strength and ability to fight, most girls do not engage in a great deal of physical fighting or overt forms of aggression. So rather than physically expressing the anger that they are feeling, girls instead learn strategies to manage their anger via much more covert and manipulative ways.

The unfortunate outcome is that girls may not learn effective communication skills to get their needs met in healthy ways. It is very difficult to tell someone something that they do not want to hear or to tell another person that something they said or did was hurtful. It can be much easier to simply spread a rumor or even cut a person out of our lives. Equally as unfortunate is the way in which many girls move through their adolescent and young adult years and still fail to develop the communication skills that allow them the freedom to speak their mind and openly share their thoughts and ideas with others.

Reflection: How do I manage conflict?

Consider the ways that you generally manage conflict. What behaviors do girls see when they watch you handle a tough situation? Consider some of the following scenarios. What do you do when:

- someone cuts in front of you in line at the coffee shop?

- someone forwards you a nasty e-mail that a coworker wrote about you?

- you hear gossip about another person who works at your school?

- a coworker makes fun of another's appearance?

- the office is planning a happy hour but doesn't want to invite one person?

- your daughter tells you that her best friend's mother thinks you are superficial and controlling?

The way that girls see adults manage conflict influences how they will approach similar situations. Providing girls with effective role modeling on how they can handle difficult and uncomfortable situations can help increase their ability to appropriately and confidently stand up for themselves and resolve conflicts in healthy and assertive ways.

The girls who have trouble speaking their mind often turn into adult women who continue to lack assertive and direct communication skills. Women then can fail to be effective role models for girls on how to communicate without being manipulative or relationally aggressive (Brown, 2003). An extreme example of this is seen currently on various reality television shows. Women are portrayed in relationships with one another as isolating, manipulative, backstabbing, and just plain mean. From the "Real Housewives" shows to "Mob Wives," "Basketball Wives" to "Love and Hip-Hop," girls are inundated with depictions of women's relationships as competitive, dramatic, and divisive.

I was recently speaking to an auditorium of sixth and seventh grade girls in an urban school district. I was talking about how difficult it can be for girls to be good friends to one another and even for adult women to be good friends. I asked the girls if they had seen the show "Basketball Wives" and nearly every girl in the room raised her hand as having seen the show. If you are unfamiliar with the show, it is essentially about several women who have boyfriends, husbands, ex-boyfriends, ex-husbands, or lovers who are in the National Basketball Association. The women on the show argue, fight, demean, and degrade each other (generally these fights and arguments are connected in some way to the men) while they simultaneously demonstrate for young girls what women's relationships with other women may often look like.

The staff and principal at the school were amazed that girls this young were tuning into a show so clearly designed for adults. But the reality is that girls are exposed to adult content in music, movies, magazines, and television, and they are looking to adult women in their lives and in the media for the protocol of what it means to be a girl. The challenge lies in that there are few effective role models in any of these venues for girls, and there are even fewer examples of effective and supportive female relationships for girls to observe.

DO WE CONTRIBUTE TO THE PROBLEM?

Unfortunately, the media is not exclusively to blame for how girls learn to relate to one another. Girls pay attention to the adult women in their lives to learn how to engage in relationships with other girls and women. As adults, we continue to struggle to have authentic and communicative relationships. We still find women who are competing with other women for the attention of men, who demean and undermine one another in an attempt to make themselves look better and who judge one another in very intense ways. While conducting a focus group of mothers with teenage daughters, one mom shared the following with me:

I think that most women have a few close female friends that they can talk to and be honest with about things. But I also think that the majority of women can't stand other women. When I was growing up I just couldn't stand to hang around other girls. I thought they were full of drama, and I would rather have hung out with guys instead. You just don't have to deal with all of that petty drama with guys. I admit I don't feel safe around other women. I feel like I always have to keep my guard up, because I am not sure when they might turn on me. I learned that strategy when I was in middle school and I've kept my guard up ever since. I think it is easier to just keep everyone away, than it is to let them in and wait to see if they are going to screw you. —Tanya, mother of a seventh grade girl

Research has identified and isolated the role that mothers can play in the perpetration of their daughters' girl bullying behavior. Specifically, they found that mothers who engage in relationally aggressive behaviors with their own friends such as gossiping, excluding them from activities, and talking about them behind their back, have daughters who engage in these same kinds of behaviors. Additionally, it has been found that mothers who have a more permissive style of parenting and seek to be their child's friend as opposed to their child's parent also have daughters who are more relationally aggressive (Werner & Grant, 2009). This is not to say that mothers are solely responsible for the relationally aggressive behavior of their daughters; rather, it is to illuminate the fact that mothers have a significant influence on their daughters' development.

Relational aggression is, yet again, one of those things that does not necessarily go away just because we grow up. The patterns of communication that we learned during our early years tend to persist throughout our adult lives. For many women, this means the absence of strong and supportive female relationships. As girls go through school and their focus shifts to boys and dating behavior, many abandon their female relationships for dating and intimate relationships with boys. They often proceed through their high school, college, and even adult years with few close relationships with women. They sacrificed their female relationships for relationships with boys, and many never recover these relationships. For some girls, college or adult life may bring them back to effective and supportive relationships with other women, but for others these relationships continue to be competitive and strained.

The challenge lies in the fact that we know that girls and women who lack effective and supportive relationships with other girls and utilize their dating and intimate relationships with boys for all their emotional and intimate support are at an increased risk for being involved in a violent dating relationship (Chesler, 2009). Girls and women need effective female relationships and we need to teach girls how to have these relationships during their early years.

Activity: Help girls identify their support systems.

Girls say that they often feel alone and that no one understands what they are going through. They report difficulties in their relationships with other girls and can feel isolated and misunderstood throughout the lonely adolescent years. Helping girls identify the people in their lives who love and support them is a critical task that can have lasting implications. Girls need to be able to picture the people in their lives who they can go to for support. Work with girls to identify:

- someone they can tell difficult things to.
- someone who can make them laugh.
- someone who always believes them.
- someone who they can trust.
- someone who really listens to them.
- someone who will protect them.

I've asked hundreds of girls why it is that they think girls don't get along well with each other. Overall, the responses of girls from all different backgrounds, ethnicities, ages, environments, and walks of life are markedly similar. They report that the girls are in competition with one another and are eager to see another girl fail. Girls make statements such as: "Girls like to see a cat fight and just want to have drama," and "Girls are in competition with one another," and "We just want to be better than other girls." These are not messages or ideas that are innately female or genetically part of being feminine, rather these are ideas that girls embody as they learn what it means to be a girl.

IMPACT OF RELATIONAL AGGRESSION

I guess I've always been a bit of a bigger girl. I mean, I'm not fat, I'm more athletic. I think I am really strong . . . stronger than my brothers. There has always been a part of me that wishes I were smaller and shorter. I don't really like being so tall. I always feel like a giant around my friends. They wear super cute little clothes and my mom always makes me wear shorts that go almost the whole way to my knees, I look like such a dork sometimes. I know that other girls always make fun of me and my clothes—they say I look like a lesbian. They call me fat and make pig noises when I walk by. I hate going to lunch because I feel like they are always watching and criticizing what I am eating so I hardly eat anything and then I am starving all day. I guess the worst was about two weeks ago. We were in the locker room changing for gym class and two of the girls started messing around with me and making fun of me. I tried to ignore it, but then they picked up my shirt off of the bench and screamed to the whole room, "Yup—size extra-large! Just as we thought!" I was so embarrassed and I didn't know what to do, so I just played it off like it didn't bother me. —Malaysia, seventh grade

The impact of relational aggression on its victims is significant. Girls who experience social and relational bullying from their peers have negative academic, social, emotional, and mental health outcomes. They often do not know who to talk to about what is happening and they feel embarrassed to report the incidents to an adult (Raskauskas & Stoltz, 2004). Girls don't want to be perceived as tattletales and so, instead of telling someone about what is happening, they act like it didn't really bother them that much. Like Malaysia stated above, she just played it off. Deep down inside she feels terrible, but the face that she must project to her peers is that it is, "no big deal."

The following lists some of the common issues seen among girls who have experienced relational aggression and, while this is not an exhaustive list, it provides a starting place for beginning to identify girls who may be experiencing this type of aggression.

Academic	Social	Emotional	Mental Health
• Decreased school functioning • Desire to skip school or avoid peers • Negative academic outcomes	• Social maladjustment • Difficulty making and keeping friends • Peer rejection	• Stress • Loneliness • Decreased self-concept or confidence • Withdrawal from peers and family	• Depression • Anxiety • Somatic complaints • Suicidal ideation

Source: Merrell, Buchanan, & Tran (2006).

Perhaps most importantly, peer victimization and aggression influence the self-concept and self-worth of girls (Merrell, Buchanan, & Tran, 2006). The experience of relational aggression can shake the core of a girl and make her question everything that she says or does. What is most difficult about this is that when a girl's confidence gets compromised during the adolescent years, she may not regain her confidence again until adulthood—if at all.

WHAT CAN WE DO?

Is it possible to intervene and change the course of girls' relationship and communication styles? I think without a doubt the answer to this question is a resounding yes! We can't just resign ourselves to the idea that girls are mean and there's nothing we can do about it.

There are concrete ways to impact relational aggression between and among girls. Part of this requires attention to the girls who are participating in the relationally aggressive behavior as well as to the girls who are victims of girl bullying. At different times, all girls can be perpetrators, victims, or bystanders of relationally aggressive behavior.

☆ **Include relational forms of aggression in the definitions and discussions of bullying and cyberbullying. Ensure that students, parents, teachers, and administrators understand the severity and impact of relational aggression on its victims**

Because of the recent emphasis on bullying in schools, coupled with the lack of inclusion of relationally aggressive behavior in many of the definitions of bullying, many parents, counselors, and educators lack a fundamental definition of relational aggression. Relational aggression is a form of bullying and the consequences to perpetrators should be applied accordingly. Relational forms of aggression should not be viewed as "girls being girls" and deemed as less severe than other forms of aggression.

☆ Teach girls about empathy and how to "walk in someone else's shoes"

Provide girls the opportunity to develop a conceptual under-standing of the fact that we don't always know what's going on in someone else's life—we don't always know their story or what they might be dealing with outside of school. Girls can sometimes judge one another on physical appearance, clothing, socioeco-nomic status, and a variety of other external factors without taking into consideration the reality of another's life. Having girls identify times when others have been empathetic toward them and times that they have demonstrated empathy to another allows them to begin to develop social competence around iden-tifying and invoking empathy. Empathy must be practiced on an ongoing basis, so it is important to give girls the opportunity to identify situations where they can demonstrate understanding and concern for somebody else.

☆ Teach girls that they don't have to like everybody, but they have to demonstrate respect for one another

We should not attempt to teach girls that they need to like everyone that they meet and that they should be friends with everyone that they interact with. (If we are being honest with our-selves as adults, we don't like everybody. We should not expect any different behavior from the girls in our lives.) Rather it is much more important that we teach girls how to demonstrate respect for others, even people that they don't really like. We do not need to like everybody, but we need to show them respect.

☆ Teach girls that not everybody is going to like them, and that's okay

Sometimes we say or do things that other people don't like and we may be criticized for doing so. It is only natural for us to want other people to like us, and for adolescent girls this pressure is even stronger. Prepare girls for the invariable fact that when they do stand up for themselves other people in their lives may not appreciate it, particularly those people who are used to bullying or controlling them. In any relationship, when we stand up for ourselves or speak to the other person in any new or different way, it changes the dynamics of the relationship. This is often a hard concept for girls and women because as girls we learn that it is important to be liked. I recently worked with a college student, Trisha, who had grown up in a family where she was the "pleaser." She was responsible for doing everything perfectly and was the one who kept the peace in the family at all costs. She never had a strong opinion about anything and could easily be directed by her family or friends to do whatever they wanted her to do. She told me that if everyone around her was happy, then she was happy, so she would go to great lengths to ensure the happiness of the people in her life. I asked her to share with me a time that she could remember when someone in her life got mad at her. Trisha could not think of a single example of a time or situation where someone was mad at her! This was an indication to me of a young woman who had an inability to speak her mind for fear that someone "won't like her," and unfortunately, this proved to be the case because Trisha had been repeatedly taken advantage of in a variety of different ways throughout her adolescent and young adult years.

☆ Teach girls the difference between passive, aggressive, and assertive communication

We have found that one of the most powerful activities we have done with girls that resonates with them for years after our programming is teaching them the difference between passive, aggressive, and assertive communication. These tend to be terms and definitions that many girls are unfamiliar with and they generally don't realize that there are different and explicit ways of communicating. Girls need to learn that there are appropriate times for passive, aggressive, and assertive types of communication. It is important that we teach them how to differentiate between and among the types of communication and when each is best utilized.

Passive:

Many girls, like Trisha, are extremely passive and have great difficulty speaking their mind or giving an opinion. The result tends to be that these individuals are easily taken advantage of and believe that everyone else's opinion or ideas are more important than theirs. They are girls who have difficulty having their opinions heard or letting others know when their boundaries have been infringed upon. People learn to be passive for a variety of reasons. This may include being the peacemaker in a chaotic family structure, negotiating fighting between a mother and father, experiencing aggressive or authoritative parenting, having a lack of self-confidence, or experiencing abuse. Passivity is a learned response to external conditions and exists to try to maintain the peace or the calm in often chaotic relationships. Extremely passive people rationalize that it's easier to go along with something that they don't agree with or easier to ensure that they don't "upset the apple cart" than it is to speak their mind. Some might say that their opinions just aren't that valuable, or that they don't really care enough to speak up. I always ask girls, "When there is something that you really want to say and you don't say it, who do you get most upset with?" Invariably, we get most upset with ourselves when we don't speak our mind and we don't allow our voices to be heard. But for many girls this internal frustration or anger is easier to manage than another person's anger, frustration, or disappointment in them. Passivity can be a long-term and engrained response to a variety of different external situations and it can be very difficult for an individual to change their passive behavior or passive style of communication. Unfortunately, we know that girls who are passive and have difficulty standing up for themselves are at risk for a multitude of negative outcomes, including lack of equity in friendships, manipulative dating relationships, negative self-worth, low self-esteem, depression, and anxiety.

Aggressive:

Conversely, we also struggle with the issue of dealing with very aggressive girls. Angry, physically intimidating, and verbally abusive girls are equally, if not more, problematic than girls who are passive. These girls attempt to rule the social hierarchy and dictate the behaviors of those around them. They respond to conflict or confrontation with an extremely aggressive response. They have difficulty engaging in effective conversations or participating in problem-solving activities because their aggression is unmanageable. What I found to be most interesting about aggressive girls is that they believe that they are standing up for themselves and "not getting taken advantage of" by other people. They perceive their behavior as a means to getting their own needs met. Unfortunately this aggressive behavior rarely produces the desired outcome.

Assertive:

Teaching girls how to communicate effectively makes common sense; however, most girls and even most adult women find assertive communication a challenge. Standing up for yourself in a respectful and confident way sounds much easier than it actually is. Telling somebody something that they don't want to hear is actually quite a bit more difficult than it sounds. This could be as simple as telling your friend that you need the five dollars back that they borrowed or telling somebody that they cut in front of you in the line in the lunch room. It would be so much easier to complain to your friend, "Oh my gosh, I can't believe she just cut in line. . . . She is such a jerk." than it would be to say, "Excuse me, you just stepped in front of me in the line. The line actually ends back there."

☆ Teach girls how to appropriately use "I" statements

Using "I" statements is a significant part of communicating assertively. We cannot expect others to read our minds, so we need to utilize our expansive communication skills to be able to tell others what we want, what we need, and how we want things to happen. This does not mean that we are dictating the terms of every relationship that we have; rather, it means that we are communicating effectively and in a reciprocal way with the people in our lives. "I" statements are simple statements that are easy to use; however, even most adults have not adequately mastered the use of assertive communication and "I" statements.

The critical element of the "I" statement is that you teach girls to accurately name the behavior that is distressing, connect the behavior to what they are feeling, and then tell the other person what they need from them.

"I" Statements

"When you _____,

I feel _____."

"I need you to _____."

☆ We must prepare girls for the responses that they may receive from others when they stand up for themselves for the first time

In our society, assertive women are not always viewed with the highest regard. When girls and women stand up for themselves, it challenges the social norms that exist around girls being quiet and passive. I have often heard girls tell me that the first time that they stood up for themselves to someone who was harassing them or trying to take advantage of them they were called a "bitch." For girls who've never been called a bitch before, this initial reaction can feel startling or discomforting. For girls who experience relational aggression on an ongoing basis or have difficulty standing up for themselves, they may need to learn that when they stand up for themselves, they might get a negative reaction from others. Talk to girls about what possible reactions they might get, and help prepare them for an uncomfortable response.

☆ Provide girls with opportunities to be in girl-only spaces

It is not often that girls have the opportunity to be in spaces that are female only. It is even less often that girls have female-only spaces where they can explore the issues facing their lives and try out new skills and behaviors. Because adolescents tend to have the belief that they are completely unique and their experiences are exclusively theirs, it is hard for them to understand that other teens their age are experiencing the same, or very similar, things. One of the most surprising things to me has been the fact that after participating in girls' programming, a number of girls will say, "I love being in the girl-only group! It was neat to see that other girls my age are going through the same things as I am. I didn't really realize that." It's not just putting girls in a room together and having them talk about their issues that is beneficial. While the mere sense of shared experience is powerful, the desired outcome is that girls develop new ways of interacting with each other and their environment as a result of bringing them together. This is where the purposeful engagement of an activity or an intervention can be most powerful. You create a safe space for girls to engage with one another, and then you provide them the opportunity to develop a new skill or competency that they can try out safely in that space.

☆ Bring girls who are different from each other together in purposeful and intentional ways

It is of little importance whether or not girls are already friends with each other when they are in a group with other girls. In fact, it's probably more beneficial to have girls who are from different groups, different cliques, and different backgrounds to all come together to have the opportunity to share their individual experiences and learn with and from one another. Girls come to understand that while they are unique, their experiences may be more universal than they realize and often girls find they have a great deal in common with other girls.

CHAPTER 4

Boys, Dating, and Danger

Guys want you to do things that you might not be ready for, but you know that if you don't do it, they will just go on to the next girl who will.

—Maya, seventh grade

Why does it seem that adolescent girls turn boy crazy overnight? I have talked to so many parents who say something such as, "I don't even know what happened to her. It is like she was one girl one day, and then woke up the next day and I didn't even know who she was anymore. She has become obsessed with her clothes, how she looks, meeting up with boys on the weekends, and sending texts that she doesn't want me to read. She spends hours doing her hair and changing her clothes, and she is trying to wear so much makeup that she looks ridiculous. I send her back upstairs to wash her face. I just don't get it. I remember being a little bit like that when I was a teenager, but that didn't happen until I was much older. She is 12 years old. . . . I am sure I was 15 when I started caring about that stuff."

DEVELOPMENTAL ISSUES

The National Institute of Health (2012) reports that girls start puberty between the ages of 10 and 14 years old, with most girls in the middle of puberty around age 12. While the age of puberty onset has declined by several months over the past 40 years, girls are starting the physical puberty changes such as breast and pubic hair development around age 9½ or 10 for Caucasian girls and as young as 8 years old for African American girls. With menstruation not far behind, girls are gaining weight, developing breasts and hips, and physically looking more womanly at younger ages. These hormonal changes mean that girls are also dealing with sexual feelings, confusing urges, mood swings, and emotions that they have never experienced before.

As girls' bodies change, their hormones race, they feel awkward and self-conscious, and can become overly concerned with their changing appearance. When girls spend hours in front of the mirror obsessing about every pimple on their face, how their clothes fit, and whether or not they look "hot" in their new jeans, we must recognize that they are simultaneously experiencing societal pressures to fit in and look a certain way as well as physical and hormonal changes that impact their physique, thinking, and emotions.

An additional impact of this early maturation is that girls start to receive sexual attention at younger ages and begin to develop sexual interest and curiosity. As adults, we can have a difficult time recognizing (or admitting to!) this reality and, in turn, we rarely prepare girls adequately for the physical, emotional, and social changes that are coming their way. Fifth-grade girls tell us that puberty is one of the big issues facing girls their age and they don't feel like they can talk to their parents about what is going on.

I have a colleague who was talking with a small group of seventh-grade girls about girls' development and the onset of puberty. As she explained to the girls, in medical terms, the process of menstruation, one of the girls actually fainted. She passed out. She had to go to the nurse's office to get calmed down and settled. While it is concerning that this was clearly the first time the girl had heard this information, what was more distressing is that some of the teachers in the school were upset and concerned that the girl had been traumatized by the conversation and the explanation. How much more traumatized could this young lady have been if she had gotten her period and did not know what was happening to her body?

Providing girls accurate information on the changes that the female body naturally experiences can help ease their anxiety and can also help them realize that what is happening to them is normal. The body changes are normal and the sexual interest is also normal. So when girls become preoccupied with dating at very young ages, it is connected, in part, to the physical and hormonal changes they are experiencing.

IMPORTANCE OF DATING RELATIONSHIPS

With these hormonal changes comes an internal and external pressure for girls to flirt, date, seek sexual attention, and engage in romantic relationships. Girls begin to see relationships as a type of social status and experience pressure from their peers to date, have a boyfriend, or be interested in boys. While some girls are exploring their sexuality and orientation during adolescence, my research found that issues surrounding boys and dating was near the top of the list of concerns for girls in all grades, beginning in fifth. There is a tremendous emphasis on the significance and impact of relationships with boys. Starting in late elementary school, boys become highly regarded as a big issue in the lives of girls. Among fifth-grade girls we hear comments such as,

"Boys are wanting to kiss on you and you want to look pretty for boys."

"We start dating and having boyfriends at this age, and our parents think that we're too young for that, but they just don't understand."

"We like attention from boys and it is really important to have a boyfriend."

Eighth graders tell us:

"We have feelings and urges and we can't really talk to our parents about that." "Like about sex. Parents just tell you don't do it. . . . But they don't understand how hard it is. They don't know what we have to deal with every day."

"I think dating is one of the biggest things that our parents don't understand. I know it was really different when they were our age, but right now everyone is dating. And if your parents won't let you then you just have to sneak around behind their backs."

By twelfth grade, the tone of girls' comments about guys and dating changes somewhat because girls tend to have more steady relationships during their later years of high school; however, they continue to have reservations about talking to adults about their concerns. They say,

"We are making decisions about whether we'll go to college near each other or if we'll just break up."

"By this point we start getting more serious with guys, and our relationships are getting more serious. Parents just think that we are going to meet someone new in college and I don't think that is always true. Some of us are in love with the person we are with right now."

"Parents are sometimes so hard to read. It's like they want you to tell them everything that's going on in your life, but when you tell them a little bit they freak out and go crazy. So you learn real quick that you can only tell them certain things . . . but make them feel like you're telling them everything."

It can be hard for adults to understand the importance that girls place on dating and relationships throughout their adolescent years. We often look at these early relationships as silly or juvenile, but for girls, the emotions are intense. Girls have shared with us at length the pressures that they feel to date, have a boyfriend, and engage in sexual activity—there is nothing juvenile about these issues.

I'm sure we've all seen it: the seventh-grade girl who's had her heart broken for the first time. She's crying, emotional, and can't seem to eat or sleep. She's doodling in her notebook swirling letters with her name and his name together with hearts. She's seeing how her name looks with his last name and trying out her signature with Mrs. . . .

As adults, we recognize the girl may be hurting and upset in a situation like this, and we do want to soothe the emotions that she has. However, we often fail miserably at our attempts in doing this. Have you ever told a girl: "You're going to meet another guy; he was a jerk anyway" or "There are other fish in the sea. When you get to college, you will meet some really nice guys. . . . I didn't meet your father until I was in college."

Unfortunately, this is one of the worst mistakes we can make. By making statements that focus on the future, we fail to acknowledge the intensity of the girl's current emotions. She doesn't want to hear that in two years she's going to meet a guy who's better. She just wants the pain that she's feeling right now to stop.

I did use the word *pain*. It can be difficult for adults to look at adolescent emotions, particularly around dating relationships and equate intense words such as pain to them. We look at their youthful relationships and see them as innocent and fun. We see their emotions as childhood emotions; however, for the teen who is experiencing them, they feel intense and, at times, overwhelming.

We've got to remember that the experience that the teen is having at this very moment may very well be the most intense emotion that she's ever felt. We cannot relate to their situation from our older and more experienced perspective, with our multiple relationships, as well as our age and wisdom. Girls do not have the luxury of looking abstractly at the situation and thinking, "This isn't so bad. . . . I'm sure I will have to deal with more difficult things when I get older." Rather their brains are saying to them, "I may not make it. I've never cared for somebody so deeply. My world has just been shattered."

When, as adults, we lose the perspective of what it feels like to be in that place of adolescence and how difficult relationships feel in that space, we become irrelevant to the lives of teens. The first time that we tell them what they feel is silly, stupid, or juvenile may be the last time they share their feelings or emotions with us. While it can be difficult for us to relate to what they're going through from our adult perspective, we can relate to them on what it feels like to be hurt, betrayed, embarrassed, or sad.

Don't tell teens that you know how they feel. Tell them that you're sorry that they're hurting. Tell them that you want to understand how they feel and that what they are going through sounds really hard. Inside you might be thinking, "This is the silliest story I've ever heard. I can't believe she's crying this much over this stupid guy," but outside you're saying, "Wow, that sounds really difficult. Tell me how you're doing."

DATING INTENSITY = COMPETITION

Girls learn from early ages that their social capital comes, in part, from their dating relationships with boys; thus, many girls seem to be constantly seeking to be part of a relationship. The obvious result of this is that girls begin to compete with one another for the attention of boys. One school counselor told me, "I think the root of all girl drama is a boy. Usually the boy is manipulating two girls, making them feel like the other one is the problem. Because girls are groomed to be pleasers, they are willing to take on the responsibility of being "the problem" in the relationship and then they will work on changing themselves so that the boy will choose *them* over the other girl."

Let me share with you a recent conversation that I had with an eighth-grade girl, Sarita:

A Conversation with Sarita: An Eighth-Grade Girl

Me: It seems like girls have a hard time getting along with each other. Do you think that is true?

Sarita: I totally think that is true. Girls are drama and just look for reasons to fight, argue, and get in each other's faces. Girls are always competing with each other.

Me: What do you think girls are competing for?

Sarita: Boys. Everyone wants the boy to like them. If a guy is giving you some attention and then starts to pay attention to one of your friends, you get pissed off about it.

Me: Who do you get pissed off at?

Sarita: At your friend. She knows that he was talking to you and she was just trying to get in there and mess it up. Guys always do that, they are going to talk to whatever girl will do what they want them to do.

Me: Tell me what the guys are looking for the girls to do.

Sarita: Everything. Guys want girls who have perfect bodies and sexy clothes. They want girls who will drop everything to pay attention to them. I think guys are also looking for girls who will do other stuff with them too . . . you know, like sexual stuff . . . send them dirty pictures and stuff. I heard some boys talking about "hitting it and quitting it" and I just don't think that is right.

Me: Ok, so let me make sure I've got this straight. Girls compete with each other for the attention of boys, but then sometimes the same boys can be pretty disrespectful to the girls. Does that sound about right?

Sarita: Yeah, I guess so. Sometimes I think that boys are one way with you and then they are a totally different person when their friends are around. They will be all sweet and nice, and then when they are in front of their friends they act like they don't even know that you are around. I think boys our age are very immature. They don't know how to treat a girl. I think that's why lots of girls look for older guys to date.

For many girls, the adolescent years are comprised of a tremendous emphasis and focus on dating, and social status is based on who has a boyfriend and who does not. This is where a connection between self-worth and romantic relationships can begin to develop. Girls do begin to compete with one another for boys' attention at very early ages, and realistically, the competition does not stop when girls become adults. As one school counselor said, "Girls try to outcompete other girls for boys. While adults may see this as being childish, we must admit that adults still deal with this and compete too! We need to listen to girls and help them define a positive body image and also define what they actually want in a relationship."

When a girl's identity and sense of self is connected to her dating relationships with boys, this can be a very tumultuous situation. We may begin to see frantic attempts at maintaining the relationship and an over involvement in keeping a boyfriend. Often this can be where we see placating or desperate behavior from girls who feel a strong pressure to have a boyfriend or be in a relationship.

LEARNING ABOUT RELATIONSHIPS

Many of the expectations and patterns of dating, as well as our coping strategies for managing conflict in relationships that we learn during our adolescent years, remain into our adult relationships. While the dating and romantic relationships of our youth generally dissolve over time, the understanding of how relationships work, and what our role is in a relationship, can impact our future dating and intimate relationships. Unfortunately teen relationships are often characterized by anxiety, jealousy, loneliness, desperation, and dependency. We also observe high levels of exclusivity and a great deal of social dominance (Sears & Byers, 2010).

Tumultuous patterns of dating during adolescence often lead to similar patterns of dating in college and adulthood. Contrary to what some parents say, locking our girls up until they are 30 years old is not the way to help them learn the skills to effectively manage dating relationships!

We have to teach girls the realities of navigating the dating world. When girls report that their dating relationships begin as early as fifth grade, it is important that these conversations start early so that the girls are best prepared to manage what they will invariably face as they get older. Girls are going to be pressured by their peers and by their dates, and our job is to make sure they are equipped to deal with this pressure.

We start this process by knowing the signs of healthy and unhealthy relationships and talking to girls about these signs while they are young. One sign of a potentially unhealthy relationship is when one person pressures the other person to do things that they don't really want to do. The pressure can be related to lots of different things, but commonly it is connected to sexual behavior, drinking and doing drugs, going to parties and hanging out with an older crowd, and lying to parents about their activities. Sometimes girls are called "babies," "immature," or "frigid" when they resist some of these pressures.

For many girls, having a boyfriend can be more important, in their minds, than staying true to their own principles. It is critical to teach girls that a person who cares about them should not want to make, or coerce them, into doing things that they don't really want to do. Providing girls the opportunity to identify the areas where they are likely to feel pressured, prior to being in the situation, gives them the opportunity to define their boundaries and identify effective strategies for handling these types of situations. The challenge here is that this requires having the conversation before the situation arises.

Activity: Starting the Conversation

Adults say that they have difficulty starting conversations with girls about issues related to puberty, dating, and sexual activity. We've got to acknowledge that there may be embarrassment or discomfort and then we have to forge ahead. Here are some ways we might start a conversation:

- "I noticed that a lot of girls in the fourth grade are starting to wear bras and makeup. What do you think about that?

- "I was watching a show on TV last night that showed these grown-up women fighting with each other over the same guy. Why do you think women do that?"

- "I'm thinking that sometime you're going to experience a guy who is gonna want to push you to go further sexually than you think you want to go. Let's talk about some things you might say or do if you are in that situation."

- "I've been hearing a lot about guys asking girls to send them naked or revealing pictures and videos on their cell phones and then when they break up the pictures get spread all over the school. Have you seen anything like that happen?"

HELPING GIRLS IDENTIFY SIGNS OF AN UNHEALTHY RELATIONSHIP

Unfortunately, unhealthy dating behaviors are much more prevalent that we might imagine. A 2011 research study found that nearly 30 percent of college women reported that their dating relationships in high school contained some violent or controlling behavior (Kaukinen, Gover & Hartman). We want to help girls learn the difference between a healthy, equal relationship and an unhealthy or controlling relationship. This can be a much more difficult task than you might think because so many of us think of unhealthy relationships as ones that are physically violent. While physical violence is definitely unacceptable in relationships and certainly a sign of an unhealthy relationship, there are also more subtle forms of control that girls need to know are equally unacceptable.

Some girls have come to expect control, domination, and violence in relationships because that is what they are exposed to in their families, communities, and in the media. I was working with a group of ninth grade girls and we were discussing the signs of an unhealthy relationship. We talked about the 2009 assault of singer, Rihanna, by her boyfriend, rapper Chris Brown. One of the girls told me, "I don't think Rihanna was completely innocent in that. She had to have done something that made him mad. I heard she grabbed his cell phone and tried to call the police and then grabbed his car keys and sat on them. She should have realized that was just going to make him mad—she shouldn't have done that." Others in the group agreed, that yes, Rihanna did something to bring the violence on herself. It was clear to me that these girls had learned that there is a level of violence that is acceptable in a relationship and that girls should keep their behavior in check so as not to upset their partner.

Other girls learn that when people are dating or married to one another they do have control over one another and are within their rights to exert this control at various points. A fifth-grade girl told me, "My mother is so annoying, if I were my dad I would lose my mind. She is constantly texting him, asking him where he is, and when he is coming home. She calls him like 100 times a day, and then she gets all mad at him when he tells her he still has some work to finish up before he can come home. I've also seen her call him when she is paying the bills and she'll be like, 'You spent $50 on gas last week and you didn't tell me.' Sometimes I feel like she is bored, so she needs him to come home and be bored too. If I were him, I wouldn't want to come home."

These are two examples of how we can use physical violence or more subtle control in relationships to make other people do the things that we want them to do. While one seems much worse than the other, controlling behavior of any kind is unacceptable. We want to instill in girls the fact that they can develop reciprocal, equal, and healthy relationships and we want them to understand what this can look like.

Let's take a look at some of the common signs of relationships that could potentially be unhealthy, or become unhealthy.

#1: He always wants to know where I am and who I am with

There is a natural interest and curiosity surrounding the person that we're dating. We want to learn all about them and we also have a tendency to want to know where they are and who they're with. When the casual "What's up? What are you up to?" turns into a perpetual and constant "Where are you? Who are you with?" we need to pay attention to these signs. While this does not describe dating violence, it is a red flag for controlling dating behavior.

We want girls to know that if the other person has a constant need to know who they are with and what they are doing and gets upset with them on a regular basis, this could be a sign of a controlling person. There are very few people who have the "right" to know every thing about you. This includes where you are, who you're talking to, and what you're doing at every moment of the day. In fact, depending on your age, there is arguably no one who should know all these things at every given time.

As we get older, our rights to privacy increase. While it's important that parents, teachers, and other caring adults have information to keep teens safe, it's also important that girls are able to define their own boundaries and the access that they provide others in their lives. I've heard many girls say, "I just don't get it; it's like he gets mad when I am hanging out with my friends or when I'm having a sleepover with my girlfriends. It's like he needs to know where I am at every minute of the day and if he doesn't like one person who's in the group, he gets mad at me."

Teaching girls that they have a right to privacy, and a right to a personal life, is a critically important step. However, do we as adults actually believe that teens have a right to privacy? Often parents have so much information on where their teen is and what they are doing (and rightfully so!) that the teen can have a hard time differentiating among who actually gets access to this information. If we observe a teen meticulously describing which friends they are hanging out with, what they are doing, and who they are with, and go into excruciating detail as though to justify their behavior to their dating partner, we need to be mindful of the potential controlling behavior that may be present.

#2: He wants the password to my phone and my Facebook account

A current trend is for dating partners to have access to one another's cell phone, e-mail, and Facebook passwords. It is seen as a sign of affection and trust that both can log onto the other's account and essentially track their communications and behaviors. Unfortunately, once again, this does not allow a teen, or an adult, to develop a sense of individual privacy. Monitoring behavior and communication is once again a sign of control. So-called equal partners in a dating relationship should not maintain control of one another. Additionally, access to technology for today's teens often produces catastrophic results once teens break up.

#3: He gets mad when I hang out with my friends

Spending time with friends is an important part of the social development of teens. Boys and girls in dating relationships are often eager to spend large amounts of time with one another. However, when the expectation is that all your free time will be spent with the dating partner and little, if any, time will be allocated to friends, there could be cause for concern.

Getting mad when the other person wants to spend time with their friends indicates an individual with high levels of insecurity and high levels of control. The difficulty here is that girls will often forgo their friendships with other girls when they start dating relationships with boys. As one tenth-grade girl stated, "I just hated to see my best friend get a boyfriend; we used to do everything together, and now I hardly ever see her. It's like she just dropped me once they started dating. And I've seen her do this before and she thinks I'm just gonna be here for her when they break up. But I'm not having that happen to me again. If I'm not good enough for her now, I'm not gonna be good enough for her when they break up. I don't understand why you can't have a boyfriend *and* a best friend and that be okay."

As mentioned earlier, girls who lack relationships with other girls and who look to have all their emotional and intimate needs met through their dating relationships are at a higher risk for being involved in a violent dating relationship (Chesler, 2009).

#4: He keeps track of where I am with my phone's GPS

With modern technology, the ability to know another person's whereabouts at any given time is possible. GPS-enhanced phones, tracker locating systems, and location and notification services provide information to another person about where an individual (or at least their phone) is located. Marketed initially as a system for monitoring children, GPS tracking has evolved into a way to keep tabs on teenagers, dating partners, and spouses. This, along with location services, social media check-in points, and geolocation photo tracking via smart phones, provides a great deal of detail on a person's activities throughout any given day. We need to teach teens about the safe and effective use of these technologies, while equipping them to set boundaries around what information they share and what information they allow others to access.

#5: He criticizes my appearance

Criticizing another's body shape, weight, size, or appearance can be a sign of an unhealthy relationship. Putting another person down, making jokes, or criticizing them can be emotionally destructive. To a girl's fledgling sense of self-esteem, negative comments about her body from her dating partner can leave real and substantial scars. As one girl stated, "He always tells me that he thinks I'm pretty, but he thinks I need to lose a few pounds. He calls me chunky. He makes comments about how pretty other girls are and how I would be so much prettier if I was thinner. It makes me really self-conscious and makes me not want to eat when I'm in front of him. He makes these comments about me when we are in front of his friends too and it's really embarrassing."

#6: I feel like I have to "tiptoe" around him so that he won't get upset

For girls, the tendency to be a "pleaser" can further compound negative interactions in already strained relationships. For many girls and women, "keeping the peace" is their role within their families or relationships. They try hard to ensure that the other person is happy, even if that happiness comes at their own expense.

If you recognize that a girl is "tiptoeing" around in her relationship with the dating partner, it is a good sign that she has some fear that upsetting him will in some way negatively impact the relationship. This often means that she won't share her authentic self, or her authentic feelings, for fear of losing their relationship. She, in essence, will put the needs of her partner before her own needs and will maintain this dynamic throughout the relationship. This then becomes the expectation of her behavior.

When this happens, it makes it more difficult for her to speak her mind or share her opinions for increased fear of upsetting the other person. For lots of girls, they feel that they are so lucky to have a dating partner that they will go to great lengths to keep the person in their lives, regardless of the sacrificing of self that has to take place.

#7: He asks me to send nude or revealing pictures or videos to him

An unfortunate trend among teens (and even adults!) is *sexting*, or sending nude or sexually explicit photos via cell phone to dating partners. While the sexting rates of teens vary from less than 15 percent in some studies to over 65 percent in others, girls report that they sext for a variety of different reasons. Sixty-six percent of girls who have sexted say it is to be flirtatious, 52 percent say it is a sexual present to a guy, and 40 percent say it is as a joke (Lipkins, Levy, & Jerabkova, 2010). Girls report that they receive frequent requests from guys to "send a dirty pic" and that they often feel pressure to do it or else the guy will just move on to another girl who will. Often girls send the photos of themselves with little thought to what might happen to the photos after the intended recipient views them. When teens break up, the photos and videos often get sent to everyone in the entire school. A recent example of this happened when an eleventh-grade girl made a sexually explicit video of herself and sent it to a classmate who was her boyfriend at the time. When the relationship ended, he sent the video to the entire football team at the school, and within days, it went viral throughout the high school. School staff, parents, and even the police became involved in the situation. Possessing or distributing nude or sexually explicit materials involving minors can be considered possession or distribution of child pornography—a felony. Administrators were not sure how to handle the situation or how to discipline the students. Parents were mortified, and the girl who was in the video was beside herself with embarrassment and depression. She ultimately withdrew from school. There have been other cases in the news about young women who have committed suicide in the aftermath of a sexting incident.

More recently teens are using Skype, ooVoo, or other computer programs that are used for video chatting and sending video messages, to engage in sexual exploration with their peers. While there may be a record that a "call" was made, teens may perceive that there is not a record of the activity or content of the call. As technology advances, it is important to know what pressures girls may be under to engage in this type of sexualized activity. While some argue that sexting and video chatting are merely technologically savvy ways of exploring adolescent sexuality, girls need to be aware of the very real potential for exploitation that is often a result of engaging in such behavior.

#8: I try to make him look good in front of my friends so they don't think he is a jerk

Sometimes when girls are in difficult relationships and their friends recognize the deficits, they go out of their way to express how wonderful and fantastic their partner is. "Oh, he's so sweet; he put a note in my locker this afternoon." "He loves me so much and bought me flowers, candy, and a card for Valentine's Day." "He's just so thoughtful; he remembered that I had a big test today and sent me a special good luck text." Granted, all these things are really sweet, but when placed into a context of patterns of behavior that are compensatory, or trying to make up or cover for the bad or controlling behavior, we see girls attempting to normalize their relationships to their friends. Their logic is that if they show everyone how wonderful and caring he is, their friends will overlook the other behaviors that aren't so attractive.

Part of this is a need to save face with her friends and part of this may be due to a girl trying to convince herself that her relationship is healthier than it actually is. My gauge of this behavior is to consider whether or not a good deed by a dating partner is as important, or as special, if it happens and we aren't allowed to share with others. For example, if we get a dozen roses delivered to us at work does it feel different than if we get a dozen roses delivered to us at home? If no one is there to witness the sign of affection, does it still feel the same? Sometimes it seems that our need to promote our relationship to others is our attempt to convince ourselves or our friends what a fantastic person we're with.

#9: He won't talk to me when he gets upset; he just ignores me

Often when girls think of unhealthy dating relationships, they think exclusively of physical intimidation or threats. However, there are nonphysical ways to control someone else's behavior and one of those is through utilizing the "silent treatment" or "giving someone the cold shoulder." Instead of talking about what it is that is bothering them, the other person will ignore their partner for a period of time. Generally, this results in the person who is being ignored trying to figure out what they did to upset the other person. This more subtle form of manipulation ensures that the person being ignored knows that they did something wrong and also learns not to do it again.

#10: He says that if I ever break up with him he will kill himself

Finally, when one partner threatens to leave the relationship and the other person is so distraught that he or she threatens to harm him- or herself, we must recognize this as a very scary form of manipulation. This puts pressure on one person to try to fix the situation so that the other will not harm themselves. Staying in a relationship because we fear that the other person is unstable or may kill themselves is not a good reason for maintaining an unhealthy relationship. However, it is a strong force of control, because no one wants to believe that they did something to make another person hurt or kill themselves.

It is important to take all suicidal threats and behaviors seriously; however, relationships cannot be maintained on the basis of this type of behavior. Generally it's not until middle school, high school, and beyond that adolescents and even adults will make these kinds of threats. The messages can be confusing as well. Should I be flattered because he cares so much about me?

Will anyone ever love me this much? It is important that girls recognize that this kind of behavior is controlling, and that the person who is making such threats may have more substantial behavioral or mental health issues.

WHAT CAN WE DO?

☆   **Provide opportunities for girls to learn about their changing bodies and to ask questions in a safe, low-risk setting**

If you work with elementary or middle school aged girls, they likely are interested in talking about their bodies and the changes that are happening. When we give girls the opportunities to ask questions and explore, we are amazed at how much they don't know about puberty! One school counselor who runs groups with girls told me that she passes out index cards to the girls before the lesson and they are allowed to write down any questions that they have about puberty and what is happening to their bodies. She then collects the cards (without any names or identifying information) and addresses the girls' questions within the group. More often than not there are lots of girls who have the same questions.

☆   **Help girls differentiate between healthy and unhealthy relationships**

Girls generally do not have an opportunity to discuss the characteristics of healthy relationships and only think about physical violence as a "deal breaker" in a relationship. I have heard so many girls say, "If he ever laid a hand on me we would be done. No questions asked." I hear fewer comments from girls regarding the more subtle yet controlling behaviors discussed above. Allow girls to explore and identify the things that are important to them in relationships without telling them what is right or wrong and allow them to decide for themselves what they will accept or not accept in their relationships. Provide a checklist that includes some of the items discussed above so that they can determine if their relationship is healthy or unhealthy.

☆ Teach girls how to set boundaries, practice refusal skills, and stand up for themselves in dating relationships

Girls and women have a difficult time standing up for themselves in a variety of settings but perhaps most often in romantic relationships. Help girls understand that the feelings of both people in the relationship are of equal importance and that neither person gets to dictate the terms of the relationship. One of the hardest things for a girl to do is to say "no," or "I don't want to do that," or "I'm not cool with that" to a person that she likes or cares about. The result is that girls often end up going along with things that they don't want to do for fear of upsetting the other person. Girls need to think about their boundaries and limits and practice saying "no" when they are not in the precarious situation so as to increase their ability to say "no" when there is more pressure to say "yes."

☆ Educate girls on the issues surrounding sexting and posting revealing pictures online

We must recognize the intense pressure that girls can feel related to presenting themselves as sexual objects (Walker, Sanci, Temple-Smith, 2011). From posting suggestive photos on their social media profiles to sending revealing photos via text message, girls mistakenly believe that this behavior will endear them to potential dating partners. As girls seek to construct their own sexual identities during their adolescent years, they are pressured by others to conform and fit in. Unfortunately, modern technology ensures that digital photos and online postings can remain long after the person who posted the photos actually deletes them. There are some effective public service announcements (PSA) online that encourage teens to "Think before you post" as well as news reports and case studies of teens whose lives have unraveled after a sexting incident gone awry. Use these videos and stories as a starting place to discuss with girls the immediate and long-term implications of digital communication. Immediate concerns are the social, legal, and psychological consequences, which include the potential impact on their futures. While it can be difficult for girls to consider the jobs, careers, and relationships they will hold as young adults, the reality is that employers may search online for content related to their prospective employees and even request that individuals pull up their Facebook profile during job interviews. Engage girls in these conversations early to prevent a poor decision during adolescence from impacting them for years to come.

☆ Help girls identify trusted adults that they can talk to about these issues

It can be difficult for girls to know who they should talk to when they feel confused, pressured, threatened, or unsure of themselves. Many do not want to tell their parents about bad things that have happened to them or the concerns that they have for fear of upsetting or disappointing them. This can leave girls feeling very alone. If they don't think they can talk to their parents, who else is in their support system? Some of these people could be: grandparents, aunts, pastors, teachers, counselors, principals, or coaches. Help girls create a list of the people that they trust and could talk to about difficult issues.

☆ Acknowledge that it can be very hard to leave a controlling or abusive relationship

You may be working with girls who are involved in unhealthy relationships or who live in a home where there is an unhealthy relationship. It is important that we don't make statements such as, "Why haven't you broken up yet? I don't know what you are waiting for." It is extremely difficult to get out of an abusive relationship, and many girls are fearful for their physical and emotional safety so they stay in unhealthy situations. This is why it is so critical that we give girls the tools to identify the signs of a potentially unhealthy relationship while they are young so that they have awareness and can make decisions about their relationships as they mature.

CHAPTER 5

Looking Out for the Girls

Identifying and Preventing Sexual Violence

About 30 percent of girls will experience some type of sexual violence at some point in their lives. We must instill in our girls that they are worth defending and that they have the capacity and the right to successfully defend themselves.

Sexual violence may be one of the scariest things for parents, educators, and counselors to think about when it comes to the girls that they care deeply about. This chapter might be the easiest one to skip because most of us have difficulty believing that our lives could be impacted by sexual violence. We often think that sexual violence is something that happens to someone else . . . to *those* girls . . . to people that we don't even know. Unfortunately, the reality is that most of us do know people whose lives have been touched by sexual violence, whether or not they have ever shared their experience with us. If you are an educator or a counselor, there is a strong statistical probability that you have encountered many individuals who have been victims of a sexual crime. In the United States, estimates range from one in three girls to one in ten girls who will experience some type of sexual violence by the time they are 18 years old. Among college women, nearly 30 percent reported that they experienced sexual violence from a dating partner while they were still in high school (Smith, White, & Holland, 2003), and about 12 percent of high school girls say they were forced to have sexual intercourse at some time in their lives (Centers for Disease Control, 2012). It is hard to think that for every classroom of 30 girls there could be three—or even up to ten—girls who have experienced or are experiencing some type of sexual violence.

A sexual violation is one of the most intimate violations that can happen to a person and is an assault that can have lasting consequences. Unfortunately, many of us lack a sound understanding of what sexual violence is and often do not have accurate information on how to identify a sexually violent situation. The Centers for Disease Control and Prevention defines sexual violence as follows:

Sexual violence is divided into three categories: (1) Use of physical force to compel a person to engage in a sexual act against his or her will, whether or not the act is completed; (2) attempted or completed sexual act involving a person who is unable to understand the nature or condition of the act, to decline participation, or to communicate unwillingness to engage in the sexual act, e.g., because of illness, disability, or the influence of alcohol or other drugs, or because of intimidation or pressure; and (3) abusive sexual contact (Centers for Disease Control, 2007).

Many of us think of sexual violence as violent, forced sexual activity or rape, when in fact sexual violence includes *any* unwanted or coerced sexual activity (Dichter, Cederbaum, & Teitelman, 2010).

Examples of Sexual Violence:

- Unwanted sexual touching (touching a person's genitals, buttocks, or breasts; forcing someone to kiss or touch another person)

- Forcing another person to perform a sexual act (undressing, posing for photographs, genital or oral contact, oral sex, intercourse)

- Pressuring, coercing, convincing, or tricking someone to engage in sexual activity

- Engaging in sexual activity with a minor (the age of consent to sexual activity varies from state to state, so it is important to know what the laws in your state say regarding sexual consent)

Often when we think of sexual violence, we think of an adult woman who is wearing a short skirt and is accosted in a dark alley by a stranger. Unfortunately, 44 percent of victims of sexual violence are under the age of 18 and the highest risk for sexual violence for girls is between the ages of 14 and 18 (Centers for Disease Control, 2012). This is the age at which we begin to see girls participating in dating, partying, experimenting with drugs and alcohol, and being exposed to higher risk situations. This is often the age at which girls are initially pressured into sexual activities and can be taken advantage of by others who may exploit their vulnerabilities.

Conversations about sexual abuse and sexual violence do not occur with any regularity and many perceive the subject as taboo. It is easy to believe that sexual violence happens to "those other people" but not in my school or community. Unlike other forms of child maltreatment, sexual abuse occurs with similar frequency in urban, suburban, and rural areas to children of various races, genders and socioeconomic statuses. Educators, counselors, and parents find it extremely difficult to talk to children about sexual violence and report not knowing what to say or how to approach the topic (Hinkelman & Bruno, 2008). When I surveyed teachers and counselors about their training to identify and address issues of sexual violence, most reported that their college training programs spent little, if any, time discussing the topic.

We learned that few adults have accurate information on how sexual violence happens, and most believe that their daughters are well-insulated from risk. Parents generally believe that their supervision of their children is so intense that there are no opportunities for an unwanted sexual incident to take place. As one parent of a 12-year-old said,

"She is almost never by herself, so there is really no opportunity for her to get into trouble. I make it my job to ensure that she is safe."

A father of a 13-year-old girl told me,

"My daughter is not allowed to date, and if she spends any time with a boy it is when I, or another adult, is around. We would not ever allow her to be in a situation where she could get hurt or make a bad decision."

Similarly, girls report that they don't drink, they don't make out with boys, and they dress modestly so they do not perceive themselves as potential victims.

"I think about what I wear and how I act so that I don't give boys the wrong message. I see girls who are wearing clothes that are very sexy and girls who are always flirting with or doing stuff with guys. I don't do any of that stuff and that is how I keep myself safe."

ISN'T IT ENOUGH TO SAY "DON'T TALK TO STRANGERS"?

When my colleagues and I teach sexual violence prevention workshops, we begin by asking the girls to discuss some of the things that we know about people who take advantage of others in sexual ways. Girls will say things such as: "He's crazy," "He has low self-esteem," "He's scary and creepy," or "He's mentally ill." Girls are generally surprised to learn that none of these things may actually be true. The one thing that we do know about people who commit sexual assault is that, almost all the time, the sexual aggressor knows the person that they assault. That means that our ideas of a scary guy jumping out of the bushes and abducting and raping a woman are usually way off base. This is especially true for girls, who are most likely to be sexually assaulted by a family member, friend, date, or someone they know and even trust.

Children and teenagers are sexually assaulted by people that they know 93 percent of the time. In these cases, about 34 percent of the time the perpetrator is a family member and 59 percent of the time the aggressor is an acquaintance. In fact, only 7 percent of the perpetrators are strangers to the victim (U.S. Department of Justice, 2000). So the idea that we only need to teach girls to stay away from strangers fails to account for how sexual assault actually happens to girls. From childhood through their teen years, girls are most likely to be sexually assaulted by a family member or friend of the family. Because few elementary aged girls are "dating," their exposure to potential abusers tends to occur within the family system or within close proximity to the family (such as a coach, neighbor, family friend, etc.). In instances where the abuser knows the victim, there is often the presence of *grooming* behavior. Grooming refers to the actions of the abuser who works to gain the trust of the child, and often her parents, in order to have increased access to her and authority over her (McAlinden, 2006). This is generally a gradual process of gaining trust through giving attention, buying gifts, and creating secrets. Kids begin to develop a loyalty to the adult such that, when the abuse begins, the child feels confused and fearful but also dedicated to the abuser. This is one of the ways that child sexual abuse persists for many years without the child reporting it to another adult or the authorities (Hinkelman & Bruno, 2008). Another of the main reasons that prevent children from reporting is because the victim often feels some responsibility for the abuse.

SHE WAS ASKING FOR IT: ADDRESSING VICTIM BLAME

One of the most difficult aspects in talking about sexual assault and violence in girls' lives is the pervasive thinking that girls and young women have some responsibility for an assault that happens to them. I often hear adults make comments such as, "She needs to watch what she is wearing. She is sending the wrong message to the boys" or "What did she think was going to happen when she went to that party by herself?" Even girls can be extremely critical of one another when it comes to sexual assault. One tenth-grade girl shared the following:

"I know this one girl whose uncle has been having sex with her for like two years. She hasn't told anyone else but me, and I secretly think she likes it. I mean—that's nasty—if she didn't like it she should just tell him that she's not going to do that anymore . . . or tell her mom or a teacher or something."

This type of thinking, called victim blame, places some of the responsibility on the victim for the sexual assault rather than on the perpetrator. As a society we tend to have very rigid ideas surrounding who is a sexual abuser and who is a victim. Several studies have shown that up to 59 percent of mental health, law enforcement, and school professionals often attribute some of the responsibility for sexual abuse to child victims. Researchers have also found that teachers tend to attribute more blame to victims than do social workers, school counselors, and school psychologists (Ford, Schindler, & Medway, 2001).

The following are a few scenarios to help you gauge your own reaction to situations where some type of sexual violence occurred:

Case #1: Amanda and Kandice

Amanda and Kandice are friends and classmates in the eighth grade. Both girls are quite athletic and play softball and basketball on the school teams and also on local traveling teams. Kandice has had a huge crush on Amanda's older brother, Chad, who is in eleventh grade. Amanda thinks Chad is a jerk and sees that he treats his girlfriend horribly and she can't understand why Kandice has absolutely any attraction to her brother. Amanda gets really annoyed when Kandice constantly flirts with Chad and, as Amanda says, "acts like a ditz" when Chad is around.

After a weekend softball tournament, Amanda and Kandice are at Amanda's house getting ready to go to a dance at the school that evening. Amanda's parents are not home, and Chad is "in charge" of the girls until the parents arrive. Amanda is completely annoyed at Kandice because she thinks that she is "throwing herself" at Chad. Kandice is laughing way too hard at his jokes, play wrestling with him, and generally being friendly and flirtatious with Chad.

After Kandice gets out of the shower, Amanda takes her turn. Kandice is in Amanda's room in a robe and is brushing her hair and picking out her outfit for the dance. Without warning Chad bursts into Amanda's room looking for his sister and finds Kandice there— completely startled and somewhat embarrassed. Chad realizes that no one is around and says, "Wow, Kandice . . . I've never seen you quite like this." He smiles at Kandice and looks her up and down. She doesn't know if she should feel flattered or embarrassed, so she smiles nervously clutching the front of her robe. "You don't need to close that—let me just have a look, I've always thought that you are such a cute girl," Chad says. Kandice is overwhelmed by Chad's sudden attention toward her and really can't believe that he is interested in her! She says playfully to Chad, "I can't do that—you better get out of here!"

Chad takes a step toward Kandice and she doesn't know what to do. He leans in to kiss her and simultaneously opens her robe and fondles her breast. She is exhilarated and panicked at the same time! Kandice has only kissed one other person, and that was at a party during a silly game with her classmates. . . . This was very different and she wasn't sure how she felt about it. Kandice shakes her head and pushes Chad away, but he pulls her in close to him. He fondles her buttocks and then traces his hand down in between her legs. She jumps away from him and rushes out of the room. Chad follows and catches her in the hallway and says, "Kandice, you are more grown up than I realized. I'd like to see more of you, but we need to keep this between the two of us, ok?" Kandice doesn't know what to do, so she smiles and nods obediently.

Case #2: Macy and Zoe

Macy is an eleventh-grade girl who looks a bit older than her age. She is popular and outgoing and generally does well in school. Her older sister, Zoe, is a sophomore in college and invited Macy to spend the weekend in the dorm with her. Macy was so excited to be spending the weekend on a college campus and hoped that Zoe would take her

(Continued)

(Continued)

around the town and to a couple of parties. On Saturday night, Zoe and Macy were in the dorm getting ready to head out to the party. Both girls were in party mode and were having a few drinks while they were getting dressed. Zoe gave Macy a minidress to wear and helped her with her hair and makeup. She commented that Macy looked like a college girl and that the guys were going to be all over her! These girls were ready for a party!!

When they arrived at the party Macy noticed that there were way more guys there than girls. The girls got in free and got plastic bracelets that meant they could drink free all night. While Macy had been to many high school parties where alcohol was present, this was her first experience at a college party so she drank slowly at first and took in the scene. Lots of people were dancing and some were in another part of the house playing drinking games. Macy and Zoe began dancing with the rest of the crowd and shortly thereafter a few guys came up to dance with them. Both girls were dancing in openly sexual ways and grinding with the guys. As the night went on, Macy could tell that the one guy, Trevor, was really into her. She couldn't believe it—a college guy was paying attention to her!

Trevor was touching Macy all over as they danced and she was enjoying the attention. He made sure that her drink was always full and at one point, Zoe looked over and saw Macy and Trevor making out in the corner. Macy was clearly enjoying herself and seemed to be totally into this guy. Trevor takes Macy by the hand and leads her upstairs away from the other partygoers. He says, "Let's go somewhere a little more private and quiet." Macy is feeling the effects of the alcohol and wants to continue kissing Trevor. She follows him up to his bedroom where they sit on the bed and continue making out. He starts to unbutton her dress and she pushes his hand away as she continues to kiss him. His hands continue to wander over her body and begin to make their way up her inner thigh under her dress. Macy laughs nervously and pushes his hand away again. . . . "Stop it, Trevor!"

Trevor responds to Macy by saying, "Baby, you've been teasing me all night. You are looking so good in that little dress; I just couldn't wait to get you up here and get that dress off of you." Macy is feeling a little nervous at this point and is wondering what she has gotten herself in to. She doesn't resist when Trevor further

> *unbuttons her dress, but when she realizes that he plans to have sex with her she freezes. "Stop Trevor, I can't do this. I need to find my sister." He tells her to relax, that he's not going to hurt her, and once they are finished he will take her back to her sister. Macy doesn't know what else to do, so she doesn't do anything.*

Self-Reflection

1. My initial reaction to each of these cases is _____

_____

_____

_____

2. If I were working with Kandice, the first thing I would tell or ask her is _____

_____

_____

_____

3. If I were working with Macy, the first thing I would tell or ask her is: _____

_____

_____

_____

When you read each, did you initially identify each place along the way that Kandice and Macy could or should have done something differently? How easy it would be to say to Kandice, "Why didn't you yell at him and tell him to stop as soon as he came in the room?" or "You should have hit him when he tried to kiss you!"

We could tell Macy that she was irresponsible for going to a college party while she was in high school and that it is illegal for people under the age of 21 to drink alcohol. We could point out that she was wearing a revealing dress, making out with Trevor, and essentially leading him on or "sending him the wrong message."

The unfortunate reality here is that both Kandice and Macy were sexually assaulted—they were part of sexual activity that was not consensual. While it seems easy for us to examine these cases after the fact and identify all the seemingly wrong things that each girl may have done, the fact remains that another person overstepped their bounds and took advantage of the girls' vulnerabilities. While there may have been actions that both Kandice and Macy could have taken, neither is responsible for the behavior of the other person and neither should carry the burden of responsibility for the assault.

What if Chad apologized and walked out of the bedroom when he realized that Kandice was not fully clothed? What if, after Macy told Trevor to stop, he said, "Oh—I thought we were on the same page here, I didn't realize you didn't want to do this" and then he stopped pressuring her? It is likely that these situations would have ended very differently. Sexual violence happens because there is a person who is willing to commit the assault, not because there is flirting, leading on, alcohol, or any other host of variables that are often, wrongfully, attributed as causal factors.

Victim blame can be a particularly hard concept for us to come to terms with, particularly because it is easier for many of us to think that *we* would respond differently in each case—that *we* could have easily prevented the situation from happening. Unfortunately, most victims of sexual violence also blame themselves for the assault. Take, for example, the following statement from a young woman, Carrie, who was sexually abused by a soccer coach when she was a teenager. Even as an adult she struggles to not blame herself for the abuse.

I was 14 when he started paying attention to me. He was probably in his 30's at that point and he was married with a baby. I looked older for my age and really hadn't been in any relationships before. I had kissed maybe two boys up until that point but never anything else. I would see him every week at soccer practice and it started with flattering comments about my body and how sexy and curvaceous I was. At 14, I didn't know what to do with that! It was exhilarating and confusing at the same time and I found that I liked the attention and wanted it to continue. I was really attracted to him and wanted him to like me, but I didn't know what to do when he started to touch me. I mean, there was a part of me that really liked it, but then there was another part of me that knew it was wrong and that it had to stay as a secret. No one could ever find out because I should have stopped it from the very beginning. I should have told him that he needed to stop and that I was going to tell an adult what was going on. I should have reported him to the school. But I couldn't—I knew people would ask me why I didn't do something right away; I let it go on for years. I knew they would say that I could have stopped this earlier if I really wanted to. I couldn't deal with that, or what my teachers' or parents' reactions would be, so it was just easier to stay quiet.

In this situation, Carrie was 14 years old and was slowly and purposefully pursued by an adult man. He clearly knew that his behavior was inappropriate and illegal yet was able to effectively manipulate the situation so that Carrie kept his secrets and subsequently blamed herself for the abuse. Unfortunately, this scenario is far too common for thousands of girls and boys and it keeps sexual abuse hidden and stigmatized.

Let's return to the self-reflection based on the cases of Kandice and Macy. Was your initial reaction to question the behavior of Kandice and Macy or to question the actions of Chad and Trevor? For many of us, our initial reaction is to pinpoint all the opportunities that the girls had to make a different decision, get out, or report the event. Our secondary response is to identify the fact that Chad and Trevor could have made different choices as well. If we are to be effective in changing the culture around sexual violence, we must be willing to shift our thinking as it relates to who is responsible for the acts.

If we are fortunate enough to be the adult in a girl's life that she will actually talk to about such a sensitive issue, we must handle her concern with the utmost respect and care. If we fail to do this, she will likely think twice before she ever confides in us again. Responses such as, "Now Macy, what did you think was going to happen when you went up to his bedroom?" Or "Kandice, do you think that was a good idea to kiss Chad back when he first kissed you—don't you think that could have sent him the wrong message?" sound paternalistic and judgmental. Girls want adults to validate their reality, acknowledge their confusion, and help them make sense of the situation. She probably already blames herself, and we do not want to add to her insecurities.

What do I say?
Suggestions for talking with girls who have experienced sexual violence

"Whatever you did to survive was the right thing to do at the time." This is the language that we use when teaching sexual violence prevention. Because survivors of sexual violence are extremely likely to blame themselves (and other people are likely to blame them as well), they will often reconstruct the situation and identify everything that they could, or should, have done differently to prevent the violence from taking place. Here are some suggestions for how we might talk with Kandice or Macy after the events:

Kandice

- I am sorry that this has happened to you. I can imagine that you felt pretty confused and you might even still feel confused about what happened.

- Sometimes it is easy for us to blame ourselves when situations such as this happen. I want you to know that even though you are attracted to Chad and may have been flirting with him that does not give him the right to touch you in the way that he did.

- You have the right to decide who can touch you, where they can touch you, and when they can touch you. Chad did not have your permission or your consent to touch you in the way that he did. What he did was wrong.

Macy

- Macy, I am sorry this has happened to you. I bet it was a pretty scary experience and a difficult place to find yourself.

- It seems like you feel that you should have prevented this from happening. I want you to know that even though you made the choice to go to the party and dance with Trevor, you did not make the choice to have sex with him. Dancing and kissing are not an invitation for sex.

CONSEQUENCES OF SEXUAL VIOLENCE

The impact of sexual violence in the lives of girls varies tremendously. Recently I read in the paper a story about a young girl who had been sexually abused by a teacher. At the sentence hearing, her parents told the judge, "She will never be whole again. He robbed her of her innocence and she will never get that back. My daughter will never have a normal life again." While I certainly recognize the horror that parents feel when they learn of a crime against their child, especially a sexual crime, I also believe that people can recover from these situations and grow up to lead healthy and productive lives. Sexual violence impacts girls in substantial ways, but I refuse to believe that the impact of this crime ruins a girl for the rest of her life. I refuse to believe that she will never have healthy relationships and that she will forever lack self-esteem and confidence. Our reactions and responses to girls who have experienced sexual violence are critically important and to communicate a lifelong sentence of pathology and doom is unfair and unrealistic. We would not want girls to believe that their lives are "ruined" and that they have no chance at a productive future.

Are the impacts of sexual violence far-reaching and intense? Yes, most definitely. Girls who experience sexual violence are more likely than girls who are not victimized to experience low self-esteem, depression, suicidal thoughts, and drug and alcohol use. Additional impacts include eating disorders, mood and anxiety disorders, delinquent behavior, risky sexual behavior or sexual acting out, and even *learned helplessness*—the belief that they do not have any control over the outcomes of different situations or relationships. If girls who have experienced sexual violence are in a relationship that is controlling or where they are fearful, they may have difficulty setting boundaries, making decisions, and being an equal partner. Girls who are involved in violent dating relationships may lack the ability to assess a healthy versus unhealthy relationship and may not have the skills or confidence to change the dynamics and expectations of the relationship, thus exposing them to the potential of being victimized in the future.

We additionally know that the greater the degree to which a person blames themselves for the assault, the worse their mental health outcomes may be and the less likely they are to tell anyone about what happened. Girls who believe that they are responsible for an assault or believe that there was something that they could have done, but didn't do, to prevent the assault have higher levels of depression, anxiety, and self-blame and they rarely tell anyone that they were assaulted. If they already blame themselves, they are afraid that others will blame them as well.

WHAT WORKS IN PREVENTING SEXUAL VIOLENCE?

Many schools and organizations are concerned with the safety of their students and implement programs that attempt to decrease the vulnerability of their students. Many programs are available that provide information and skills to students related to preventing sexual violence. As we consider such programming, we must be cognizant of what actually works, and is research based, when it comes to effective prevention programming for girls.

As soon as I began working in sexual violence prevention in 1997, I began to receive "tips" and "strategies" from friends and family members regarding keeping women safe. I can't tell you how many e-mail messages I have gotten over the years that gave directives to girls and women about ways to stay safe, avoid rape, or avoid the "wrong kind" of men. Some of the most unrealistic have included suggestions for girls to never wear their hair in a ponytail, to never park next to a white van, to always ask the security guard at the mall to escort her to her car, and to never get on the elevator if a man is on it. Unfortunately, we have no evidence that doing, or not doing, any of these things is related to avoiding sexual violence. Often the messages that girls receive on how to keep themselves safe encourage them to engage in elaborate self-protective behaviors and can provide a false sense of security (i.e., "I am headed to the mall to meet a guy I have been chatting with online. When I get to the mall, I will not park next to a white van . . . thus I am keeping myself safe."). Girls and women often develop misplaced fears in that they may be afraid to walk alone at night yet have no reservations about being alone with a date. Let's consider the actual realities of some of the most commonly heard self-protective strategies:

Myth #1: Never walk alone at night.

While this might be easier for younger girls to follow, from middle school on through adulthood, most girls find they need to walk alone at night at some point. While there is certainly strength in numbers and having girls look out for one another is great, there has been no research that correlates walking alone at night to increased likelihood of rape. The available research is to the contrary, indicating that the majority of sexual assaults occur either in the home of the victim or the perpetrator, rather than outdoors or in unfamiliar places.

Myth #2: Never talk to strangers.

Girls are only sexually assaulted by strangers in about 7 percent of cases. That means that 93 percent of the time juvenile sexual assault victims know their attacker. About one-third of the time girls are assaulted by a family member (parent, grandparent, sibling, cousin) and about 60 percent of the time girls are assaulted by friends or acquaintances (dates, family friends, coaches, neighbors, friends-of-friends, etc.). So the idea that we only need to teach girls to stay away from strangers fails to account for how sexual assault most often happens to girls.

Myth #3: Just go along with it so you don't get hurt.

A large body of research over the past 20 years has indicated that girls and women are much more likely to prevent a sexual assault from occurring if they utilize assertive resistance and protective strategies, such as physical resistance. In fact, nonforceful verbal resistance, such as begging, pleading, or crying, is actually associated with an increased likelihood of experiencing a completed sexual assault and an increased likelihood of being injured. It is important to teach girls to be assertive or even aggressive and to yell, run, and defend themselves.

WHAT CAN WE DO?

☆ Provide girls with accurate information on how sexual violence happens and how they can respond to potentially threatening situations

Girls need to learn the above myths and facts about sexual violence and recognize when they might be vulnerable. Teach girls who the most likely offenders are, as well as strategies they might use to keep themselves safe. We would use different strategies when we feel uncomfortable or pressured on a date than we would if we were confronted by a stranger. Think back to some of the assertive communication strategies that we discussed in a previous chapter on "Mean Girls." Girls can learn to use these, and other similar strategies when they are feeling pressured or threatened.

☆ Teach young girls that they have a right to stand up for themselves

Very young girls through elementary school-aged girls need to learn that they have a right to stand up for themselves. Young children are often expected to follow along with any adult directive and are not given the chance to ever say "no" or to not do something that is asked of them. Young girls should be taught that they do not have to hug or kiss people that they don't want to hug or kiss—even if the person is a family member or friend of the family. Some parents have difficulty with this and expect that children will obey them at all times. Letting girls know that people should not touch them on the parts of their body that would be covered by a bathing suit can help young girls understand what "private parts" of the body are. Giving a girl the power to set that boundary and make that decision will enhance her confidence and her sense of having ownership over and respect for her own body. By instilling this idea in younger girls, we will experience less difficulty when we expand on the information with older adolescent girls.

☆ Know the signs of sexual abuse and violence and consider the possibility that the distress in a girl's life could be related to experiencing violence

There are many different signs that we would look for if we believe that a girl may have experienced some type of sexual violence. While this is not an exhaustive list, it provides some general information on behavioral and physical indications of abuse. It is important to note that these indicators are not confirmations that a child or a teen has experienced violence; rather they are characteristics that would tell us that there is some level of distress in the girl's life. The distress could be due to many different things such as parental divorce, being bullied at school, or a behavioral health issue, but the distress could also mean that there has been some sexual violence. So our role, as difficult as it may be, is to consider the possibility that abuse could be present.

Younger Children

• Bed-wetting, thumb sucking, fear of the dark	• Sexual acting out with peers
• Nightmares	• Tension stomach aches
• Separation anxiety	• Age inappropriate ways of expressing affection

Pre-Puberty and Teenage	
• Truancy	• Alcohol or drug abuse
• Excessive bathing	• Anxiety or depression
• Withdrawn and passive	• Delinquent behavior/acting out
• Sexual inference in artwork	• Sexual promiscuity
• Decline in school performance	

Physical Indicators	
• Bruises or bleeding	• Sexually transmitted diseases
• Pain or itching in genitals	• Pregnancy
• Difficulty sitting or walking	• Frequent sore throats, urinary tract infections, yeast infections

Source: Child Welfare Information Gateway (2012).

☆ Teach girls assertive and physical responses to violence

Girls can learn simple verbal and physical responses to situations of potential threat. However, before any assertive response can be taught effectively to a girl, we must first instill in girls the idea that they are worth defending and that they are capable of defending themselves. Girls have not generally been reinforced for being strong, physical, or loud. When we teach sexual violence prevention to girls, we are asking them to push back against some of the traditional ideas about girls' strength so that they begin to experience themselves as powerful and as possessing the capacity to influence the outcome of a potentially violent situation. Even the smallest girl can learn skills that can be used on the strongest offender. Effective sexual violence prevention for girls teaches them how to exploit the vulnerabilities of a stronger attacker. As girls get older they can learn more sophisticated protective skills and can utilize different strategies in various situations. Enrolling girls in girls-only self-defense classes can help them learn and practice these skills.

☆ Provide girls the opportunity to identify their support systems and the trusting, caring adults in their lives that they could talk to about sensitive topics such as sexual violence

Girls rarely tell others when they experience sexual violence because they are often embarrassed or believe that they did something to bring it on themselves. I work with many women in counseling who were sexually abused as children, or sexually assaulted in college, who have never told a soul because of fear and embarrassment. Helping girls to identify who they could talk to if they were assaulted and who will believe them and support them, is critically important. Girls do not want to be questioned or met with suspicion if they tell another person what happened to them, they just want someone to believe them and comfort them. Sometimes the reaction of the adult can make the girl close up, stop talking, or recant their story. If we, as adults, react with horror, disbelief, or anger, then girls will be hesitant to share their experiences with us. While it can be difficult, we need to meet their disclosures with care, concern, and support.

☆ Help girls understand that adults and children should not have "secrets" with one another

One of the common ways that child sexual abuse persists for many years is that the adult tells the child that they have a special "secret" that they are not allowed to tell anyone. Often, breaking the secret is associated with threats, "If you tell anyone I will hurt your mother/kill your dog/send your father to jail" and so forth. Young children have difficulty knowing that this is a bad secret and one that they can, and should, tell another person. Talk to girls about the difference between "good" and "bad" secrets. An example of a "good" secret is a surprise birthday party. Overall, it is a good idea to tell girls that adults and kids shouldn't keep secrets between one another.

☆ Know your ethical and legal obligations

Many of us feel ill-prepared to handle situations involving alleged child abuse and feel even less equipped to work in an academic setting with students who have been sexually victimized. We often do not know what our reporting responsibilities might be and don't understand when we need to call child protective services. Some research has suggested that many school professionals lack the ability to recognize and understand the pervasive effects of child sexual abuse and they report sexual abuse cases

less often than they would if they had more and better training. School and counseling personnel need to know their legal
responsibilities regarding reporting sexual violence and protect-
ing children, and professional development opportunities can
address this information.

Educators, counselors, social workers, and other helping
professionals are mandated reporters of child abuse. This means
that if we have a suspicion that a child is being abused and we
do not report it to child protective services or the police, we can
face legal consequences. While educators and counselors are
legally required to report child abuse to a child protection agency,
any person can freely make a report if they have a suspicion
of abuse taking place. Parents, family members, coaches, and
friends can notify police or a child welfare agency if they believe
a child is being abused. Most agencies allow an individual to
make an anonymous report if there is a hesitance to identify
oneself. When addressing these difficult situations, the first step
is to know what to look for, and the second step is to know how
to intervene. The goal is to create an environment and a relationship where a child feels safe to disclose the abuse and then
the adult can take action to stop the abuse and protect the child.
Schools and organizations should have clear policies and procedures that all staff should follow regarding reporting requirements, chain of command, and documentation of all activities.
Allowing sexual abuse to go undetected or unaddressed is both
an ethical and legal issue for adults who work with kids.

CHAPTER 6

Smart Girls and Dumb Blondes

I think sometimes girls think that they should not be too smart around boys. The boys won't like you if you are too smart.

—Audrey, sixth grade girl

As I stood in the auditorium before a group of giggling and excitable sixth-grade girls, I posed a few questions. "Who thinks that girls can be anything they want to be?" Without fail, every hand in the room was raised. "Who thinks that one of you young ladies, here in this room, could be the president of the United States someday?" Once again hands rose throughout the room. Girls laughed, made jokes, poked their neighbors, and were generally excited. The next question I asked was, "Who thinks boys can be *too* smart?" The girls responded with a resounding, "No! Absolutely not." Then, "Do you think that girls can sometimes be *too* smart?" It was so interesting to watch the dynamics that happened next. Several girls raised their hands; many shouted out, "No!" Others put their hands up halfway as they looked around the room to see what their peers were doing. The girls were not sure what to make of this question, and it clearly wasn't such an easy answer.

> **"Most men ask 'Is she pretty?' not 'Is she clever?'"**
>
> —Vintage advertisement for Palmolive Soap

The idea that girls have to dumb themselves down to be liked by boys is, unfortunately, not a new idea. Several years ago, I cut out a "Dear Abby" column from the newspaper. It was written by a 13-year-old girl who said that she was a great student who enjoyed her school work. She talked about completing her assignments ahead of time and being very engaged in her studies. She said that she was at a sleepover with her girlfriends and they were all talking about where they would end up in 20 years. Her friends told her that she would not be married with a family; rather, she would be a rocket scientist instead. The young girl asked Abby, "Should I focus less on my school work and more on my social skills with boys?"

SMART = INTIMIDATING

Girls feel the pressure to be feminine, desirable, and well-liked. They recognize that "fitting in" is extremely important and they often internalize the expectations that they should be accessible and not intimidate the people around them. And for some reason, the idea of girls and women being smart has often been equated with them being intimidating. Girls, who are socialized to be nice and kind and to ensure that the people around them are comfortable, can have difficulty when they hear that they are intimidating. The idea that their brains, smarts, knowledge, and hard work can intimidate someone else can make girls feel that they need to tone themselves down and not appear *too* smart.

Many adults believe that this trend has passed, and now it is "cool" for girls to be smart; however, many girls would disagree.

I think that people look at girls and think that, first and foremost, they are supposed to be pretty. There is a pressure to look a certain way and act a certain way, and I think that girls want people to like them. That is really one of the most important things. Girls who are really into their school work get made fun of and are called, 'nerds' or 'geeks.' I think that some of us, myself included, try to see that as a point of pride. Yes, I am smart and I like to learn, but that doesn't mean that I don't like to have fun with my friends. I don't get how people think that you are either fun, silly, and stupid or that you are smart and serious and boring. —Meghan, twelfth grade

Apparently, the pressure for girls to not be "too smart" becomes a bigger concern when there are boys around. Girls have fewer concerns about being smart in front of other girls than they have when they are around boys. There is a pressure to not be perceived as too intelligent around boys, because that could be seen as intimidating in some ways. Instead of being proud of their intellect, girls often play down this aspect of themselves when they are around others.

> One of my friends is super smart and she always gets 100 percent on our assignments and tests. Our teacher does this thing where people who get 100 percent have to come to the front of the room and the rest of the class is supposed to clap for them. I know she always gets embarrassed, and I know that the rest of the class isn't really clapping because they are proud of her. They basically roll their eyes every time she gets called to the front. Last week she told me that she was going to intentionally miss a couple of questions on the next test so that she didn't get called to the front again. —Isabel, seventh grade

Hundreds of online blogs, discussion forums, and advice columns are focused on "smart girls who intimidate guys," "girls playing dumb to get a date, "how to pick up a smart girl or a dumb girl," and "hot versus smart: which would you pick?" The conflict remains for girls—you can't be both smart and desirable.

> "There is a girl I know who acts dumb to get attention, but she is really, really smart. I don't understand why she does it, because it is so annoying. She is like trying to be that dumb blonde." (Klaudia, seventh grade)

I was speaking with a group of teachers recently and several commented on the way in which very intelligent girls would play down their intelligence when there were boys around. Here is a conversation I had with one teacher:

Conversation with a Teacher: Why Do These Girls Act So Stupid?

Richard: Why do these girls act so stupid?

Me: Tell me a little bit about what you are seeing.

Richard: Ok, I work in an after school arts program with boys and girls year round. So I get to see them in an academic environment and also in a social setting. There is a group of really smart, high-achieving girls who do quite well in school. They are academically competent and get great grades.

Me: Ok, this doesn't sound so bad.

Richard: Right, that part of it is fine. The problem is that I know these girls are bright but then I see them act like they are stupid. This happens year after year. We will do small group activities and we'll put the girls into a group with a "cute" or "popular" boy, and then they suddenly seem stupid. I mean seriously stupid. They act like they don't know how to do anything, like they can't follow directions, and like the brain that they have just stopped working.

Me: Why do you think they are acting like they don't know how to do anything?

Richard: That is a great question. At first I thought that maybe it was because they wanted the boy to have to explain the directions to them, or they wanted the boy to feel like he was in charge. Then I thought that they are just looking for an excuse to draw attention to themselves or make a commotion. Sometimes I watch these girls and I feel like they will do anything to get attention. If they simply followed the directions and understood what the task at hand is, then they wouldn't have any reason to make a fuss. I guess they think that boys will pay more attention to them if they are making a fuss.

Me: So from your observations, girls will act dumb in front of boys so that they find an opening to talk to him or try to have him explain what they are supposed to be doing?

Richard: I guess that sounds right. I think these girls need to realize that being stupid is not attractive. What they are doing is selling themselves short. I just want to call them out and say, "Stop acting this way—you are so much better than this!"

I wanted to hear what girls themselves thought about being proud of their intelligence, but I knew I had to ask the question in a specific way. If I asked girls, "Do you ever act stupid in front of boys to get their attention?" I probably wouldn't get very useful responses. So instead I asked girls why they think girls are sometimes embarrassed about being smart. I didn't connect the question to boys in any way; however, the girls' responses were overwhelmingly connected to boys' opinions of them. Among sixth-grade girls, I heard the following responses to the question, "Why do you think some girls are embarrassed about being smart?"

"'Cause if you seem like you are smart, the boys will say, 'Oh you are too smart for me, you can't be my girlfriend.' They think you are a geek."

"It depends on the kind of boy that you like. If you like a certain kind of boy, you might be trying to act tough, or hard, or cute around him to get his attention."

"Guys don't want a girl who is smarter than them. They want to be in control."

Activity: Ask Girls What They Think

Ask the girls in your life about their perceptions of "smart" girls or women. Depending on the messages that have been reinforced for the particular girls, they may have a wide variety of responses to these questions. What is most important in your conversation is that you provide them with a safe place to talk about these questions. If girls feel that there is a "right" answer that you want to hear, they may limit their responses.

- I've heard that sometimes girls feel pressure to be either smart or pretty, what do you think about that?

- Who are some of your female role models that you believe are intelligent women?

- Some people think that girls can "dumb themselves down"—or pretend that they aren't as smart as they really are—when they are around guys. Is this something you have ever seen?

- How do you think intelligent women are portrayed in the media? Who are some of these women?

- Do you think girls, in general, would rather be smart or pretty?

HARDWIRED: BOYS ARE GOOD AT MATH, GIRLS ARE GOOD AT READING

What do you tell your daughter, or the girls in your classroom, when the president of Harvard University says that girls just aren't capable of doing the high levels of math and science in quite the same way as boys? In 2005, when Larry Summers, then president of Harvard University, stated that girls and women have a "different availability of aptitude" that prevents them from being as successful as boys and men in the sciences and science-related careers, he essentially told girls and women everywhere that there is really nothing they can do about their deficits; they were just born that way.

In much the same way that careers have become stereotyped into male and female categories, specific subjects in school also maintain specific gender expectations. Historically, it has been thought that boys are good at spatial tasks, including subjects in school such as math and science, and girls are good at reading and writing, and so they flourish in subjects such as English and literature.

When children are three and four years old, boys and girls perform the same on assessments of spatial skills, counting, and math computation (Eliot, 2009). Girls in early elementary school perform as well as boys in math and science. However, as they get older their scores begin to slip and the discrepancy between the genders becomes a bit larger throughout high school. By high school graduation, there is a noticeable gap on achievement tests such as the SAT and the ACT with boys outperforming girls on the math sections of the SAT and girls outperforming boys on the verbal test. But while boys have outperformed girls for over 20 years on the math section of the SAT, the gap has diminished considerably over the past several years.

As we have seen an improvement in girls' achievement tests, high school graduation rates, and college attendance rates, some social scientists, sociologists, researchers, and educators have questioned whether the gains for girls have come at the expense of boys. They suggest that if girls are doing better, that must mean that boys are doing worse and that we are experiencing a "boys' crisis." The reality is that *both* boys and girls are doing better. While girls are graduating from high school and attending college at slightly higher rates than boys, the proportion of boys who are graduating high school and going on to college is at an all-time high (American Association of University Women, 2008). Similarly, when it comes to achievement test scores, there has not been a decrease in boys' scores and an increase in girls' scores; rather, both boys' and girls' scores have improved.

There has been a great deal of sociological, neurological, and psychological research that has attempted to understand the variance between the learning and achievement of boys and girls. Some scientists argue that there are innate differences that exist in boys and girls from the time they are born that are responsible for the discrepancies in achievement in different subjects. This is the "nature" approach—that we are genetically predisposed to excel at certain things based on our gender.

Others argue that children are born as a blank slate with boys and girls being relatively equal. Every experience and opportunity that children are presented with throughout their formative years helps shape who they are, what they are good at, and what they will ultimately become. This is the "nurture" approach, which contends that we are shaped by societal influences and by our experiences.

RESEARCH FOCUS: THE PLASTICITY OF THE BRAIN

As we try to answer the question of nature versus nurture, we must consider both the biological brain differences that exist between girls and boys as well as the differences that we develop based on how we are socialized and educated by our parents, friends, media and the rest of our environment.

Biologist and scientist, Lise Eliot, PhD, has conducted extensive research on the brain and specifically, brain differences between boys and girls as well as the way that the brain grows and develops in relation to what it is exposed to and the experiences that it has. In her book, *Pink Brain, Blue Brain*, Eliot (2009) discusses the very small ways that children's brains are different, based on their gender. In her review of hundreds of research studies that looked at brain size, brain activity, differences in sensory processing, and frontal lobe development, she found that there is actually "surprisingly little solid evidence of sex differences in children's brains." The brains of young boys and girls are much more similar than they are different!

So how is it that men and women become so different that by the time they are adults there are more marked differences between their brains? Enter the term *plasticity*. Plasticity is a term that describes the way that the brain reacts, changes, and responds to different experiences. The brain is likened to a muscle that changes in response to the way that it is used. As we go through changes, experience new things, have new relationships, and develop new skills, the brain changes its structure to respond to our life experiences. Every time we do something new or experience something different, our brain reacts accordingly so that, over time, the structure of our brain is shaped by all the influences and experiences of our life.

Dr. Eliot asserts that "learning and practice rewire the human brain, and considering the very different ways boys and girls spend their time while growing up, as well as the special potency of early experience in molding new neuronal connections, it would be shocking if the two sexes' brains didn't work differently by the time they were adults."

This research tells us that the exposures we provide to girls as they grow up, and the things that we reinforce in their lives, will help shape the way that their brains develop. Through providing girls with learning opportunities, we can have the option of expanding their cognitive skills, as well as their interpersonal skills.

We know that our abilities are expandable and that learning has a significant role in our intelligence, our interests, and our personality. When we consider cognitive differences such as speaking, math, mechanical ability, or interpersonal skills such as empathy and competitiveness, we must consider the degree to which these differences have been shaped by our social learning and how these differences have been innately programmed. In other words, we must consider how our experiences impact the genetic predispositions that we have.

Most contemporary scientists look not exclusively at nature versus nurture, but how nurture influences nature—that the experiences we have, the things we are exposed to, and the interactions that are part of our lives impact the genetic predispositions that we have. This would suggest that our approach to helping girls must take into consideration the fact that their brains are moldable and pliable throughout childhood and adolescence and that despite any hardwiring that girls or boys experience, they have the ability to develop social, emotional, behavioral, and academic skills. And this ability to learn outweighs the genetic or biological predisposition that we may or may not be born with.

Reflection: Nature Versus Nurture—What Do You Think?

As you think about your own life experiences and your own academic skills and achievement, what were the big things that influenced you? How much of your academic and career decision making was connected to your genetics and how much can you attribute to what and who you were exposed to? Some of the questions you might consider are the following:

- Did you have same gender or opposite gender siblings?

- When you played as a child, do you remember building, or constructing things or taking care of, or nurturing, things?

- Do you remember reading books, completing puzzles, doing flashcards, or writing stories as a child?

- What was your parents' level of educational attainment?

- What peer group did you hang around with in school? (Were you an athlete, in the band, in the chess club, a loner? Did you skip school all the time, or were you a serious student?)

- Were you encouraged to take certain courses or participate in specific activities? (sports, dance, choir, debate, student government, etc.)

CAN GIRLS BE "BOTH/AND" RATHER THAN "EITHER/OR"?

Clearly, there is a stigma for girls around being smart. It is one that many won't readily admit to parents or teachers but is certainly one that girls recognize and internalize. For many girls, it means that you can be smart at the expense of being pretty or desired by boys. Like the young girl who wrote into the "Dear Abby" column, she was told by her friends that she could be a rocket scientist or she could get married and have a family. High achieving girls report having a difficult time negotiating their studies, their femininity, and their social lives (Skelton, Francis, Read, 2010). More simply stated, girls struggle to try to "have it all." Achieving good grades, being popular, being pretty, and being liked by boys are areas where girls say they feel pressure. Girls say that as long as you are pretty and popular, you can also be smart—that these traits (attractiveness and social skills) can "balance out" the intelligence.

This either/or thinking seems especially prevalent during the younger years, when girls are really trying to figure out who they are and what they value. When fitting in is of the utmost concern, any area of real or perceived difference can be mortifying for girls. They want to fit in and they want to be liked by their peers, and during adolescence, this can be more important than being smart or high achieving.

Case Study: "That is for boys. . . ."

I was interviewing a group of female engineers and discussing with them their own process of coming to identify with engineering as a career. I was interested in knowing what influenced and motivated them to enter such a male-dominated profession (only about 11 percent of engineers are women). Each woman spoke of their aptitude in science and math, however, they also reported that they were often encouraged by teachers or counselors to become math or science teachers. The women spoke of being only one of a few girls in their advanced classes in high school and feeling tremendous pressure to try to "fit in" and not always be the "smart girl."

One participant said, "My mother and father are both engineers, and I think that had a lot to do with me becoming an engineer as well. I had constant reinforcement from the time I was little that I was good at designing and building things and that I could become a scientist or an engineer. I remember when I was about 9 or 10 years old and I was invited to a birthday party for one of the girls in my class. My mom and I went shopping for a birthday gift and I bought my friend this very cool build-your-own-robot kit. I was super excited about the gift and couldn't wait for my friend to open it. Everything she had gotten so far was clothes, stuffed animals, and sparkly nail polish kits. When she finally opened my gift, she looked confused and disappointed and just sort of shoved it to the side.

(Continued)

(Continued)

One of the boys at the party said, 'That is a boy present, why would you give that to a girl?' I was so upset because I thought it was so cool. Then I got embarrassed and became really self-conscious about it and said, 'Sorry, my dad picked it out.'

From that day on, I found myself thinking about everything that I said or did and wondering what other people would think. I questioned the things that I was good at and the things that I liked and became embarrassed about my academic strengths and interests—I questioned whether I was doing things that people would say boys are supposed to do. In retrospect, I found that I would play down my intelligence and my curiosity so that I wouldn't stand out from the other girls. It really wasn't until I went to college and met a few other women who were really into the same things that I am that I started to feel comfortable again in my own skin. I realized that I could like what I like and that it was okay."

PROMOTING GIRLS' ACADEMIC ACHIEVEMENT

There are many factors that contribute to the academic achievement, persistence, and motivation of girls. Support from parents, peers, teachers, and counselors is critical as a girl seeks to identify her strengths and interests. When girls believe that they have support from these important people, they are more motivated to achieve in specific areas. Researchers (Leaper, Farkas, & Brown, 2012) looked at girls' participation in the subjects of math, science, and English. They found that when girls felt they were supported to excel in particular areas by the people that they care about, then girls were more likely to do well in those areas. They found that this support was most needed when girls were participating in subjects or activities that have been more stereotypically typed for boys, such as the subjects of math and science.

What is so interesting about this literature is that the researchers found that when girls are supported and encouraged in a specific area or subject (such as math, science, or English) the girls' motivation in those areas increases. When girls feel that their achievement in a particular subject is not supported by peers, family members, or teachers, their motivation for that subject decreases. Thus, general academic support and encouragement are important, but content and subject specific reinforcement may have a stronger impact.

Subject Specific Support & Encouragement

Providing girls specific and instructive feedback and encouragement can help improve their academic motivation and performance. Here are some examples of general and specific feedback:

General:	**Specific:**
You are so smart.	You are doing a great job with long division. I can see how hard you are working.
You did well on your science test.	You clearly have a solid understanding of the process of osmosis; nice work!
That math test was hard, but you did a good job.	Algebraic equations can be really difficult, but you figured it out and nailed that test. Awesome!

While parents and teachers are tremendous influencers, the importance of peers in the lives of girls cannot be overstated. Girls' friendships and social circles can have a big influence on their academic interests, persistence, motivation, and achievement. The characteristics of the friends that girls have, coupled with the girls' own characteristics, can affect how girls perform academically. Most often, girls hang around with other girls who are somewhat similar to them. They may have shared interests and attitudes and, subsequently, similar behaviors. Friends can have a mutual influence on each other, and this can be positive or negative (Veronneau & Dishion, 2011). Friends can impact school success in the following ways:

• *Problem Behaviors:* Teens who have friends who participate in delinquent behaviors such as substance use, aggression or destruction, or who have attitudes or behaviors that are inconsistent with school success, have lower levels of academic achievement.

• *Academic Achievement:* Higher achieving friends can help contribute to school success and academic achievement. If it is "cool" to be smart and girls can learn effective study and learning strategies from their peers, they may be challenged to achieve at a higher level than they would be if they had average or low achieving friends.

• *School Engagement:* Friends who are more engaged with school, follow school rules, and put effort into learning and participating can have a positive influence on their peers.

While other people are critically important influencers in girls' lives, we also know that the way a girl feels about herself can also impact her achievement. Confidence and self-concept are connected to academic achievement. In fact, self-concept and achievement are reciprocal in that each influences the other. When girls experience low self-concept and low confidence in their abilities, it is likely that lower levels of achievement will follow. Conversely, girls who have higher levels of self-concept, specifically academic self-concept, and approach school tasks with increased confidence tend to have higher achievement. Success reinforces one's self-concept and people with high self-concept achieve more. Our work with girls must focus on what we can do differently to encourage and develop them, while also focusing on what girls can be doing differently to build themselves up and to experience success in a variety of academic areas.

WHAT CAN WE DO?

☆ Teach girls that their skills are expandable

Parents will often say, "I wasn't good at math, and so it is no surprise that she's not good at math." When I learn that the child they are referring to is only in second grade, I worry that they have already written off their child's math abilities. As children grow and become more cognitively complex, they also can develop new ways of thinking and reasoning. Our skills are expandable, and while certain subjects may be more challenging, we all have the ability to learn new skills. Especially for a child so young, her competencies should not be predetermined based on the parent's perceived strengths or deficits. We want girls to know that they can improve their performance in all subjects and can learn to be better students of math, science, reading, or writing.

☆ Teach girls that smart *is* beautiful, and pretending to be stupid *is* stupid

Girls perceive that boys prefer girls who are not necessarily their intellectual equals. While this may not be the prevailing sentiment of all the girls that you come in contact with, there are plenty who do believe this—at least in part. I do meet lots of girls who are extremely proud of their intelligence and excited to put their intellectual merits on display. But I also see girls who are embarrassed about the grades that they earn and do not want to share their high grades with peers who are boys or girls. Because the need to fit in, get attention, and be liked by peers is so important for teen girls, we have to try to understand why they would "dumb themselves down" in certain social settings. For a variety of reasons, girls can struggle with demonstrating their intelligence. They are afraid to be smart because they fear the potential negative social implications. What will everyone think? Will everyone roll their eyes at me? Will the boy think I'm a nerd and pay more attention to my friend? Regardless of the "why," we must recognize that this is a legitimate, albeit sad, reality for some girls. It can be frustrating to watch girls who are actually smart *pretending* to be stupid, while the rest of the world sometimes tells them that they *are* stupid. We need to help them redefine beauty, femininity, intelligence, and confidence so they can understand that all these traits can harmoniously coexist. From very young ages, we want girls to believe that being smart is fantastic and that who they are intellectually and cognitively says more about them as an individual than who they are externally.

☆ Encourage girls to build relationships with positive and high achieving friends

Girls can have a positive or a negative influence on one another and can be highly influenced by their peers, especially during the middle school years. Helping them connect with friends who are also focused on academic achievement and success can foster their continued growth and development. It can be hard to set limits on girls' friendships, particularly when their peer groups can seem to change so rapidly, but it is important to know who their friends are, who their friends' parents are, and how their values, actions, and behaviors are consistent or inconsistent with your own. Admittedly, girls bristle when parents tell them, "It's not you that I don't trust. It's them" or "I don't know their parents; I don't think you need to spend the night." However, ensuring that girls are surrounded by positive social and academic influences can help set them up for a successful future.

☆ Refute the stereotype that certain subjects in school are better for boys or girls

Adults and teens alike continue to hold stereotypes that boys and girls are better at, or designed to do, certain subjects or tasks. When adults hold stereotypes about particular school subjects and their appropriateness for boys or girls, there can be a significant effect on students' later achievement and career choice. Interestingly, researchers have found as fathers' belief in gender stereotypes increase, girls' interest in math decreases (Davis-Keane, 2005). That means that when girls see that their dad has traditional ideas about what girls should do or be, the girls' academic performance in typically male-dominated subjects gets worse. Girls pay attention to the messages that they get from others regarding what they are supposed to enjoy and be good at from very early ages.

☆ Provide girls the exposure/ opportunity to engage in math and science supportive environments

Parents provide their sons with more opportunities to develop math and science skills than they provide their daughters. From buying math and science toys to engaging in math and science building activities, parents place greater importance on these subjects for boys compared to girls (Davis-Keane, 2005). It is then no surprise that girls become less interested, and subsequently less skilled, in some of these areas. Encourage girls to be on the robotics team, the Geek Squad, the environmental club, and the math team. Help them find girls' math, science, and engineering camps at local universities and the opportunity to meet other girls who have similar interests and aptitudes.

☆ Create a classroom environment that is safe for girls to take risks

Girls want to learn in a classroom environment that feels safe and predictable. They want to know that if they raise their hand to answer a question and get it wrong, they will not be made fun of or maligned by their teacher or their peers. Girls prefer teachers who are in control of the class and who create the space for inquiry, learning, respect, and academic risk-taking. They want encouragement and challenge, with equalized interactions between the boys and girls in the class.

CHAPTER 7

Lady Doctors and Male Nurses

Expanding Girls' Career Aspirations

People think that girls should be the ones who do all the cooking, cleaning, and taking care of the kids and that the guys should be the ones working and making money. I don't think that's right.

—Brittney, sixth grade

Girls have more options available to them than ever before as it pertains to occupational choice; however, this has not always been the case. It was only during the Second World War that women began to enter the workforce with regularity in order to assist the nation in a time of warfare. In doing so, women realized that they enjoyed, and were good at, various occupations outside of the home and at the end of the war desired to maintain their employment. Girls and women began to explore their occupational interests and found a whole new arena from which to gain satisfaction and a sense of accomplishment.

Our occupations are a part of our identity and our careers help define who we are. When we initially meet new people, invariably the question is asked, "So what kind of work do you do?" We categorize and rank one another based on these social and economic categories, and we place great importance on our work identity. Unfortunately, we do not spend very much time career planning, and some of us often view the process of career development as a sort of planned happenstance.

When you think about your own career development, what comes to mind? Consider the following questions:

CAREER SURVEY

1. When I was a child, I thought I would be a _____ when I grew up.

2. When I was in middle school, I wanted to be a _____.

3. When I started college, I majored in _____ and thought I would be a _____.

4. The career that I currently have is

    a. the worst ever. I can't wait to leave.

    b. fine for now, but I'm always looking for the next opportunity.

    c. good and stable. I know what to expect from day to day and I'm comfortable.

    d. the perfect fit for me. I can't imagine myself doing anything else!

5. The biggest influences on my career decisions have been _____.

6. My biggest regret about my career development is _____.

7. If I had known in high school what I know now, I would have _____.

How much of your own career decision making was planned happenstance, a situation where chance events and environmental factors determined your career direction? What were the interests, curiosities, life circumstances, and realities, that helped influence your career path?

When I was in kindergarten, we had a career day where each student had to choose a career and then memorize a poem that accompanied the profession. I can't remember if I was assigned this particular career, or if I chose it, but I was to be a nurse. I wore a nurse's uniform and said, "When I grow up I'll be a nurse to help you when you're sick. I'll do the best things I can to make you better quick." By the time I got to middle school, I was heavily involved in sports, so I thought I might want to be an athletic trainer. Then, once I got to college, I was convinced I was going to be a pediatrician and started college as a pre-med major. After breaking multiple glass beakers and test tubes in chemistry class and gagging while dissecting a pig in biology, I thought I might need to reconsider my career path, thus prompting my studies in psychology and education.

I've talked to many adults about their own career development. Some can easily say that they knew since they were in elementary school the career that they would have. One teacher told me, "I knew that I would be a teacher from the time I was in second grade. I never wanted to do anything else and I never even considered another career path. It was what I was meant to do." Others have less intentionality and less of a clear and direct path. One very successful business owner told me, "I started out as a high school history teacher, but I was so close in age to the students that I didn't think I would last long at that job. I quickly moved on to sales and found that it was something that I was pretty good at. I kept seeking out opportunities for promotion and increased responsibility and was successful at that for a time. But there was a point that I realized that I wasn't going to make it any further in that particular company, so I took a risk and started my own business. It has turned out to be the best decision I ever made but at the time was one of the scariest things I had ever done."

It is interesting to compare these two career paths. Both people are content and fulfilled in their work, but they had two very different paths. The teacher was female and the business owner was male. Can we draw any conclusions about gender differences in career paths?

GENDER STEREOTYPES AND CAREERS

While there is not necessarily a gender difference around early career decision making or intentionality of career path, there are gender differences that exist related to the types of careers that males and females choose. Despite great gains over the years in the occupational opportunities that are available to girls, there still exists a very strong stereotype regarding the types of jobs that are more appropriate for men or women. Read through the list of the following professions and think of the very first image of the person that comes to mind when you read each word:

- Construction Worker
- Hair Stylist
- Elementary School Teacher
- Police Officer
- Pediatric Nurse
- Truck Driver

- Computer Engineer
- Heart Surgeon
- Florist
- Secretary
- Auto Mechanic
- Stock Broker

If you are like many people, the images that popped into your mind were overwhelmingly traditional in regards to gender. While you may have had a few of the occupations listed conjure a specific person who was not of the stereotypical gender, in general we tend to have very rigid ideas about who we see in different environments and settings.

Often, this happens without conscious awareness and we find that our ideas about who does what type of job to be engrained in us as long as we can remember. In fact, it probably is as long as we can remember, because much of our career understanding and conceptualization happens during our childhood and elementary school years.

CAREER DEVELOPMENT: EARLY CHILDHOOD YEARS

Some of the early career influences for girls are related to the types of exposures that girls have when they are very young. Let's consider the types of toys that are marketed toward boys and girls. Boys' toys tend to be much more action-oriented and skill-based such as robots, Legos, Erector Sets, science kits, cars, and trains. These are toys that promote movement, skill acquisition, and spatial reasoning. Girls' toys overwhelmingly include baby dolls, ironing boards, kitchen sets, makeup, and clothes and fashion. These toys promote nurturing, caretaking, and domestic work—girls can even have a baby doll that wets itself so girls can learn how to change a dirty diaper. (See Peggy Orienstein's book, *Cinderella Ate My Daughter*, for a more in-depth review of this topic.)

While it is hard to know the impact of these activities and exposures on children, it can be reasoned that some of the earliest ideas that children develop about skills, activities, and the world of work happen during play. Children learn through play and they understand very quickly the toys and activities that are for boys and the ones that are for girls. Dolls are for girls, cars are for boys. Girls learn how to cook, boys learn how to build. Kids begin to develop their early ideas around careers when they are quite young, and so we want to ensure that their career ideas are vast and varied from these very early ages.

Activity: Take a Field Trip to the Toy Store

Take a walk through your local toy store or down the toy aisles of your local general store. Look at the various toys that are marketed to boys and to girls. What do you notice? First of all, you are likely to notice a big difference in color schemes. The girls' toys are overwhelmingly pink, but boys' toys are all different colors! See if you can find the exact same toy in a boy version and in a girl version. What colors do you think define a boy or girl version? For example, you might find PlayDoh that is available in primary colors as well as PlayDoh that is available in pastel colors.

Now, take a look at what skills you think each toy would help develop in a child. Do you see different opportunities for boys and girls?

Next time you have to buy a toy for a child, think about what you are saying to them about their roles, skills, and competencies!

CAREER DEVELOPMENT: ELEMENTARY YEARS

During their early years, there is a great deal of career education that happens for young children. Between the ages of 3 and 5, children begin to understand the concept of work and develop an early understanding of professions (Gottfredson, 2002). They understand that adults go to work and have jobs. Kids this age might start to talk about what they want to be when they grow up and will begin to identify real-life occupations rather than say they want to be a super hero, a cartoon character, or an animal.

Between 6 and 8 years old, children form an understanding of who does what type of work. At this stage the initial gender assignment begins (Gottfredson, 2002). Kids know that women are nurses and that men are construction workers. They see scientists as men in white lab coats and administrative assistants as women at a computer behind a desk.

Even at these young ages, introducing students to the idea that men or women can occupy any job can be a daunting task. Individuals tend to hold very rigid expectations about occupations and gender, and to consider men or women in careers that seem to be gender-incongruent can be difficult. One middle school counselor said,

> *When we talk about nontraditional careers for boys or for girls, I experience the "giggle" effect. It is really difficult for kids to think about men who work in salons, or as nurses, or women who are construction workers. What makes this so funny and what are we teaching them that results in this?*

This is an extremely valid question. Where do children construct their ideas about various occupations, and who does what type of job? Historically, professions have been dominated by one gender or the other and overwhelmingly careers are stereotyped as male or female. Consider the title of this chapter. I remember when I was growing up—and even still today—I would hear the following, "She's a lady doctor" or "He's a male nurse." While unnecessary, providing the gender clearly points out that the person occupying the position is in some way unusual. This type of stereotyping is damaging to both girls and boys because it limits their career options from very young ages. It makes both feel that they should not consider specific careers because they are not meant for people of their gender.

Activity: Draw a Scientist

Ask your student or child to draw a picture of a scientist. Do not provide him or her with any additional instruction and see what they draw. Next, ask the student to draw a picture of a nurse. Take note of the gender of each drawing. Use this as an opportunity to discuss gender stereotypes and careers and to dispel the myths that boys and girls can only do certain types of jobs.

I asked a group of fifth grade girls about their career aspirations. Each took a turn sharing what they thought they wanted to be when they were older. The range of responses included stylist, lawyer, fashion designer, teacher, singer, and pediatrician, to name a few. With few exceptions, girls had identified careers that were much more female dominated than gender neutral or male dominated. Next, I asked the girls if they believed there were some careers that were better suited for men than for women. There was an emphatic, "No!" followed by a, "Well . . . maybe there are some jobs men should do instead of women. Like construction and stuff. I am not saying that women can't do it, I just think that women wouldn't really like to do it." Another girl said, "I think there are jobs that people think men can do better than women, but I think we can do anything that we want to do."

It was interesting to see that at this stage, overall, girls believed that they could be or do anything that they wanted. However, most identified with more traditional careers for themselves. I conducted similar focus groups with mothers and asked them questions about their daughters' career aspirations. The mothers' responses were interesting as it became clear that many had never talked to their daughters about their career ideas. A few mothers had vague ideas of the interests of their daughters, one said, "I have never really heard her talk about anything specific." Another mom shared, "I told my daughter that she doesn't have a choice when it comes to her career, I'll tell her what she will be."

When I asked the moms about jobs that were more appropriate for men or women, their initial response was similar to the girls', "No!" followed by a, "but . . . " The "but" was connected, in large part, to the mothers' concerns about the ability to effectively manage a career and motherhood. One mom stated, "I told my daughter, 'You can be anything that you want. You can be a doctor, or a lawyer, or a CEO. . . . But just know that it will be hard to have a baby, too." Girls learn from a very early age that motherhood and career success may conflict, and this message is reinforced to them throughout their lives. On the other hand, boys may be denied the opportunity to choose fatherhood over career. Kids will reject careers based on gender incongruity before they will assess whether a career is accessible to them or a good fit for them (Gottfredson, 2002).

Activity: Who Do You Know?

This activity is designed to help girls identify real people in their own lives who have nontraditional roles or careers. Help girls identify people that they know that fit into the following categories:

1. A working mother with a child under the age of 2

2. A stay-at-home father

3. A dual-career couple who has decided to remain child-free

4. A woman who is a scientist, engineer, or IT professional

5. A man who is a nurse, elementary school teacher, counselor, or social worker

If girls have difficulty identifying people that they know, this is an ideal opportunity to have a conversation about some of the long-held stereotypes about men's and women's roles. Talk with girls about why each of the individuals named would make the choices that they have made. Ask the girls what they see as some of the challenges that each might face in their daily lives.

You might be in a more traditional role yourself. You can use your own valuable experience to share with girls how you came to your decision around your career or family role. What were the pressures you experienced or continue to experience? Is there anything you would have done differently?

CAREER DEVELOPMENT: MIDDLE AND HIGH SCHOOL YEARS

Once kids have a firm understanding of gender and gender roles, they begin to notice other characteristics of individuals and careers. Between the ages of 9 and 13, kids begin to pay attention to the prestige of different jobs. They start to recognize that there are socioeconomic differences between people and they begin to make correlations between socioeconomic status (SES), prestige, and various occupations. At this point also, teens start to make decisions about where they see themselves fitting into certain occupations based on their perception of themselves (Gottfredson, 2002). Similar to what happens with gender incongruence, when youth perceive a disconnect between how they view their own level of prestige and the prestige levels of various careers, they again eliminate some desirable but perceived unrealistic choices. Because men, overall, have more prestigious careers than women, girls have a more difficult time identifying with higher powered, higher paying jobs. Boys and girls are again narrowing their options yet probably don't even realize that this is happening.

> Overall, men have jobs that are more prestigious and higher paying than women. The U.S. Department of Labor (2011) reported that women earn about 81 percent of what men earn.
>
> An additional challenge is that while women currently make up about 49 percent of the nation's workforce, they comprise 59 percent of the low-wage workforce (people who are in the lowest 20 percent of earnings).

At ages 14 through 18, teens begin to consider internal characteristics such as motivation, values, and ability. Many begin to explore their perceptions of their own mental ability, academic skills, and determination. How hard am I willing to work for a particular outcome? What is my dream job and do I think I am smart enough to have it? If there is an inconsistency between how a teen sees himself or herself and how they view a particular occupation, the career options are further eliminated.

As adolescents go through this process, they begin to develop a sense of the level of career accomplishment that they want to have in life. Throughout the years, they have eliminated careers that don't fit the perception they hold of themselves. If I think that I am interested in chemistry or chemical engineering, but I don't see any one of my own race or gender in that field, I am likely to have difficulty seeing myself there. This, often subconscious, process results in the development of a *social space*—a zone of potential and acceptable occupational options that fits with self-concept (Gottfredson, 1997). It is essentially a narrowed set of options based on how I actually see myself.

SELF-CONCEPT AND CAREER DEVELOPMENT

We know that the adolescent years are when young people begin to make sense of who they are within the larger context of the society in which they live. Adolescents tend to have an evolving self-concept, or way in which they construct the world around them, and they are constantly seeking to make sense of who they are and where they belong in the world. For girls, self-concept declines markedly from elementary school to middle school, and then again from middle school to high school. The adolescent years are when girls' self-concept and self-esteem are at their lowest points.

If girls' self-esteem is lowest during adolescence, and a great deal of career decision making happens during adolescence, then how are girls' career decisions impacted?

In the following chart, the negative thoughts that girls have about themselves and their abilities, behaviors, aptitudes, and interests, can have a significant impact on the decisions that they make about their futures. We need to work to instill in girls a strong sense of themselves as capable and competent. We need to provide girls with opportunities to develop skills and to realize that they are good at any number of things. We need to build them up during these tumultuous years so that they are able to consider the widest range of options for their futures. Our understanding of the unique issues that affect girls' career development, specifically as it relates to self-concept, is important. With this fundamental background, we can help girls engage in the career development process with increased awareness of how their thoughts and feelings about themselves can impact their ideas around career planning.

Girls' Self-Concept	→ Girls' Thoughts	Career Decision Making
Self-concept, or the way that I feel about myself, is at its lowest point for girls during adolescence.	*"I'm not really that good at anything."*	Girls develop lowered career expectations.
Girls begin to question their abilities, intelligence, and competence.	*"I don't think I am smart enough for that career."*	Girls impose limits to their options based on the fact that they don't perceive themselves as a good fit for lots of careers.
Girls internalize societal messages about what girls can do or should be.	*"I don't see anyone who looks like me in that job."*	Girls choose less prestigious, lower paying careers.
	"I don't think I can have a family and be successful in that career."	

CAREER PLANNING

As girls begin to envision who they can be, we don't want their dreams to be negatively impacted by low self-esteem. We want girls to see themselves as successful, happy, and fulfilled in their future career. We need to provide them with the opportunity to explore their "possible selves"—or who they can be in the future.

When we encourage girls to explore what they hope, expect, or fear becoming in the future, we motivate them to make intentional academic and occupational choices. Envisioning what we want to be in the future, and how we see ourselves in the future, can guide our academic and career decisions. This is the first step in career planning—becoming aware of choices and decisions.

Career decision making is a developmental process. As girls mature, they pass through a series of developmental tasks that allows them to begin to form ideas about who they are and what they might be able to accomplish as adults. Consider career

Career Awareness and Planning Model
THINKING ABOUT YOUR CAREER PLAN

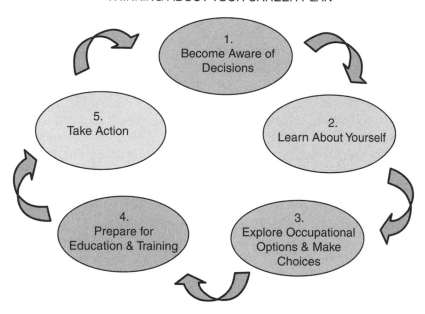

planning as a series of stages that we pass through in an attempt to make a career decision. Use the Career Awareness and Planning Model above for reference (Hinkelman & Sears, 2009).

Start with providing girls the opportunity to learn about educational and career decisions. Where do they see themselves? Will they go to college? How much money will they make? Getting a sense of the possibilities that exist is the first step in planning for the future.

Next, we want girls to have the opportunity to learn about themselves. What do they like and dislike? What are they passionate about? Some questions to ask girls include the following:

1. What kinds of things or activities do you like to do?

2. What are your favorite subjects in school?

3. What subjects seem easy to you?

4. What are the subjects in which you do your best work?

5. What do you like to do for fun or as a hobby?

The third step is for girls to explore various occupational options. There are many resources now that can provide girls with information about a wide range of careers. One of the easiest and most accessible is an online resource called O*Net (The Occupational Information Network—www.onetonline.org) O*Net is a database that contains information on hundreds of different occupations. Individuals can explore various professions and examine the knowledge, skills, and abilities that are required for each occupation. Educational requirements, salary information, and anticipated demand for the profession are included as well.

The fourth step is to make plans for the education and training that is required for the types of careers that seem interesting. We can help girls understand the importance of the academic and curricular decisions they make at the various points throughout their education. Girls can inadvertently foreclose or restrict future opportunities by the course patterns they choose in middle school. For example, girls who avoid advanced math courses minimize or eliminate their chances to pursue science, engineering, or technological occupations in the future. Encouraging girls to take the most rigorous courses that are available and then helping them be successful in those courses is very important. Girls might think it is better to get an "A" in a general math class than to get a "B" in a higher level course. But colleges report that it is better to take higher level courses and earn slightly lower grades than it is to take easier courses and breeze through with all "A's."

Some girls are now taking courses in middle school that count for high school credit. This means that the traditional idea of the ninth grade year being the year where things "start to count" is no longer true. Middle school is now where the college planning track begins, and it is important for girls and their parents to recognize this reality. Girls cannot explore or choose educational or occupational goals without relevant information and an understanding of the consequences of their curricular decisions. Mapping out courses well in advance of the next academic year is a wise and thoughtful decision. Starting this process in middle school will ensure that girls have the opportunity to take the highest level courses.

The final step is taking action. When girls register for their high school courses, sign up for a job shadow, or apply for internship experience, they are taking action. Point this out to them and continue to encourage their active participation!

WHAT CAN WE DO?

Much of the career exploration and development curricula that are utilized in schools focus on characteristics of different types of work and on individual interests, traits, and abilities. Unfortunately, these approaches to career development fail to account for the way that interests, traits, and abilities are developed and shaped in individual children. If a girl's sense of self is changing, unstable, and easily influenced during adolescence, then social, environmental, and psychological factors must be considered as we attempt to promote career development.

☆ Ensure that girls have access to a wide range of gender-neutral toys, experiences, and activities

We know that children learn through play and develop early ideas, as well as skills and competencies through their early exposures. Provide both boys and girls with toys that will allow them to develop the widest range of skills. Boys can learn to be nurturing and girls can learn to build.

☆ Broaden the horizons of young girls

Some of us may think that occupational stereotypes are no longer a problem and that girls have much broader visions of what they can do. In some instances, this is in fact the case. But many of the same stereotypical ideas about what occupations are like and what girls should or should not pursue cause many girls to undervalue their talents and skills and ignore nontraditional occupations. You can make a difference by helping girls learn more about themselves, assess their skills accurately, and explore a wider breadth of occupational options. We need to recognize the social pressures that exist for girls and work to illuminate role models and successful women in a wide range of careers. Conveying the message to girls that they can be successful in any type of career, including male-dominated careers, may inspire young women to consider occupational possibilities that they may have initially discarded.

☆ Provide opportunities for career-related internships and job shadows

Internship programs can give girls the opportunity for actual work experience and the opportunity to try out a possible occupation. Internships, co-ops, and job shadows can give an authentic sense of what it might be like to work in a particular industry and allow girls to see how it might fit with their own skills, interests, and abilities.

☆ Provide opportunities for intensive programs

Intensive summer programs can provide in-depth opportunities for career exploration and development. It gives girls the chance to immerse themselves into a field or a subject and be around others who share their interests. Many organizations, colleges, and universities offer intensive summer programs for girls. Check with your local institutions of higher education, Boys and Girls Clubs, recreation centers, and youth organizations to see what type of summer programming they offer.

☆ Connect girls with career mentors

Provide opportunities for girls to connect with career mentors who are older, more experienced people who act as role models and advocates. Career mentoring can have academic, professional, or personal functions and can be developed through formal or informal networks. Career mentors can help model or validate the career possibilities of young girls (Packard & Nguyen, 2003). Often, girls have fewer same-sex and same ethnicity work models to observe than their male counterparts. Many girls have not been exposed to women in nontraditional occupations and thus fail to see themselves as possibly succeeding in those occupations. Providing girls with opportunities to meet with female mentors who look like them and listen to speakers from nontraditional occupations are strategies that you can use to help female students begin to view themselves as individuals who can be successful in various career areas.

☆ Confront the stereotypes that girls are not good at math and science

We need to question why so many girls like science in the beginning of elementary school but have begun to lose that interest before middle school. Research supported by the National Science Foundation (2003) showed that in fourth grade 66 percent of girls and 68 percent of boys reported liking science. While the boys' interest continues, girls begin to lose interest in science by the end of elementary school. Perhaps girls are socialized to see math and science as something only boys do. Research shows that teachers' and parents' support are critical to fostering girls' interest in science, engineering, and math. Making girls more aware of the science and math-related careers that are available can influence their decisions about what courses to take in high school and lay the foundation for an engineering, math, science, or technology career.

☆ Expose female students to successful career women in nontraditional occupations

Continually, young girls endorse career aspirations that are stereotypically female, because they do not have exposure to women who are in nontraditional careers. While girls might easily have exposure to women who occupy traditional careers, there is a lack of female role models throughout the educational system and in society as a whole. Direct and personal exposure to actual women who embody nontraditional occupations is imperative to the conceptualization of various career possibilities for young women. It is additionally important that girls have the opportunity to see women who are of the same ethnicity as they are in different career roles. Having the opportunity to picture oneself in a particular job makes the possibilities seem more realistic.

☆ Conduct activities and develop support groups for girls that focus on improving self-esteem and self-concept

With the recognition that self-concept is inextricably related to career development, we can devise individual and group activities that foster self-reflection. Through an examination of the types of stereotypes that exist in our culture for women and the way in which women are portrayed in the media, girls can look within themselves to clarify what is truly of value to them and compare that to the values society holds. Activities can teach girls to recognize the ways in which media and society work to enhance girls' insecurities and perpetuate an unequal distribution of access to power. Group activities are ideal for adolescents because it gives them a safe place to express their feelings and to explore their deep thoughts and beliefs. They are able to examine self-doubts and come to the realization that they are not alone in their thought process and that their peers share the same concerns. Girls find comfort in knowing that the insecurities and pressures that they experience are not unique and often readily accept such social support (Wigfield, Battle, Keller, & Eccles, 2002).

☆ Challenge institutional and societal reinforcement of stereotypes

Promoting change in an unsupportive environment is difficult; however, maintaining the status quo can result in the lack of forward progress of students. Schools can be prime examples of the reality of gender stereotypes: Women occupy the majority of teaching and secretarial positions, while men engage in more of the powerful administrative positions of principals and superintendents. Young women need role models who demonstrate the belief that they are competent, capable, and entitled to pursue careers that may be inconsistent with those they see in their environments.

CHAPTER 8

Girls' Leadership in a Boy's World

Leadership skills help girls to capitalize on their education, express their opinions and ideas, take action on issues of personal importance, make healthy decisions, and work toward future dreams and goals.

—CARE USA Girls' Leadership Development

andering through a bookstore to check out the books that focus on leadership and leadership development, I found shelf after shelf containing books on how to succeed in business, how to get other people to follow you, how to lead for change, and how to develop effective leadership practices. There were books and workbooks on organizational culture, leadership in education, leadership assessment, and developing effective teams. There were a handful of books that focused on women's leadership, but I could not find much of anything that focused on girls.

So I jumped into the professional literature. What kind of research has been done on girls' leadership development and what have we learned about effective ways to foster leadership in girls? While there is a growing body of research that looks at women's leadership, there is surprisingly little actual research that focuses on girls. I came across popular culture articles and books, as well as a variety of organizational reports, but I was surprised to learn that there is not much out there that really looks at the evidence-based strategies to foster leadership in girls. How do you actually develop leadership skills in girls? One of the organizations that has taken the lead on much of the information and research that exists regarding leadership development in girls is Girl Scouts USA. They have conducted large scale studies to better understand the way that girls define leadership and how they perceive themselves as leaders. Interestingly, this 2008 research found that while 69 percent of girls see themselves as leaders right now, only 39 percent of girls want to be leaders in the future. What is the top reason that girls don't want to be leaders? They view leadership as incompatible with how they see themselves.

VIEWS OF LEADERSHIP

Most authors who write about leadership seem to agree that leadership, in general, is the ability to provide others with a sense of direction, a willingness and capacity to assist others in the improvement of their performance, and the ability to make up one's mind, delegate tasks, and maintain efficiency. When looking at the individual traits and characteristics that are necessary to achieve these outcomes, the research becomes a bit more ambiguous. Examining the individual characteristics and numerous models of leadership can make for a very confusing understanding of what leadership actually is—and who is best equipped to be a leader.

Our descriptions of leadership are often based on our experiences with and exposure to different types of leaders. Part of the challenge in addressing leadership development with girls and women is differentiating and isolating the actual traits and characteristics that are associated with leadership and then have girls and women see themselves in that description. Many of the concepts surrounding leadership tend to connect to traditional male models of leadership. Complete the following activity and then look at the traits that you identified as traits of leadership; which traits would you say are considered more "male" in nature, and which traits are more "female" oriented?

Activity: What Makes a Leader?

Examine the lists of traits below and write the ones in the box that you think describe effective leadership:

• Harsh	• Assertive	***Traits of Leadership***
• Inspiring	• Selfless	
• Self-Assured	• Organized	
• Meek	• Good Listener	
• Emotional	• In Control	
• Caring	• Creative	
• Decisive	• Competitive	
• Aggressive	• Visionary	
• Dramatic	• Risk Taking	
• Vulnerable	• Collaborative	
• Volatile	• Strong	
• Confident	• Makes Others Happy	
• Kind		

Generally, most people would say that girls and women are more often described as meek or emotional, and boys and men are more often described as self-assured or in control. Does your leadership box have more male or female traits? If you are like most people, including girls who were asked to identify traits of leadership, you are likely to have identified more stereotypically masculine characteristics than you are to have selected stereotypically feminine characteristics.

This stereotypical view of leadership contributes to the fact that girls can have a difficult time seeing themselves as leaders. When leadership is described using words and terms that I do not use to describe myself, and I don't see any people who look like me in leadership positions, then it can be hard for me to see myself as a leader.

Let's take a look at some of the institutions where the leaders have a great deal of influence, such as businesses, schools, organizations, and the government. We can look to some of these prominent leadership positions in our local communities to determine if they are posts that are generally held by men or if we have female leaders in these positions who can serve as role models to our girls. Use the following activity to begin to identify who holds various leadership positions in your community.

Activity: Leaders I Know

This is an activity you can complete yourself or have girls complete. It is an opportunity to identify the people who are in leadership positions in your school, organization, community, state, and country.

	Male	Female
1. The pastor/leader/priest at my place of worship is	❑	❑
2. The governor of my state is	❑	❑
3. The president of my country is	❑	❑
4. The CEO of my company is	❑	❑
5. The superintendent of the school district in my community is	❑	❑
6. The president of the college that I attended is	❑	❑
7. The mayor of my city is	❑	❑

This type of activity can be a good starting place to talk with girls about who are the people who occupy powerful positions in their communities. Are there more men or women in these roles? Are there people of their own race and ethnicity in the positions? What do they believe it takes to be successful in different types of leadership roles?

As girls begin to pay attention to people in leadership positions and develop their own perceptions of what it means to be a leader, we need to focus on the concerns that girls have about their own expression of leadership. Girl Scouts USA (2008) researchers found that girls have unease about becoming leaders and see some barriers to their own leadership development.

Girls' top concerns about leadership include

- being in charge all the time;
- getting a lot of attention;
- having a lot of power and authority; and
- having a lot of responsibility.

The barriers girls identified regarding their own leadership development include

- lack of confidence in skills and competence;
- difficulty with public speaking or talking in front of others;
- potential for embarrassment or being laughed at; and
- not wanting to appear bossy, to make people mad, or to be disliked by others.

We can easily see how girls could feel increasingly uncomfortable in taking on leadership roles if they do not feel that they have the skills or capacity to be effective leaders. The issues around low confidence and needing to be liked are major barriers to effectively standing up for oneself, let alone leading others. This information can help us determine what we need to address with girls regarding their perceptions of leadership as well as their perceptions of themselves.

EXPANDING THE DEFINITION OF A LEADER

As girls develop a firmer understanding of leadership traits, skills, and behaviors, we want to enhance the congruity between these skills and their sense of themselves.

I think when people think of leaders, they automatically think of strong, aggressive men because they are the ones that you see out there leading things. They are running the businesses, coaching the big sports teams, and basically running the country. I just don't think you would ever see a woman doing some of that stuff. Not because women don't want to but because everyone would try to stop her from doing it. I think women can do the same things that men can do, but I don't think they have the same opportunities. People still seem to think that there are certain things that men and women should do, and being in top leadership positions is not something that you see a lot of women being able to do. Unless you have grown up in a family where you were constantly told that you can be a leader and saw your mom or grandma taking leadership—if you were just sort of looking around at the world, you would automatically think that men are the ones who are the leaders and that women are the ones that support them. —Maggie, eleventh grade

We need to help girls realize that being a leader does not mean acting like a boy, being loud and aggressive, or controlling everyone around you. Girls need the opportunity to broadly conceptualize leadership and to begin to see themselves as having the potential to develop the traits and characteristics associated with various types of leadership. This means that we have to help them understand that being a leader means more than running a big company, gaining the most prestigious high-paying positions, or having influence over an entire city, state, or country.

There have been efforts over the years to expand the definition of leadership from being controlling and competitive, to being more multifaceted with an ability to inspire and to steer ahead. Organizations have recognized the value of the different leadership styles and have flourished with strategies such as inclusion, cooperation, quality control and an emphasis on collaboration (Catalyst, 2007). Some of these traits and characteristics that have been thought to be traditionally female are becoming more desirable among leaders. So the question is, do female leaders more easily embody the communicative and pleasant roles? Do they excel more in areas of interpersonal communication, relationships, and interest in other people? Conversely, are traditional masculine leadership characteristics truly the most effective? Perhaps women do possess the characteristics that are more direct and assertive, however, when they use these skills or strategies, they are often viewed as aggressive, moody, or volatile. Consider the following case study:

Case Study

You are running late for work and you have an important presentation coming up. Your boss has been on your back about this presentation for weeks and has told you what feels like 100 times that the 'bigwigs' from New York are going to be there. You are carrying your child into the daycare and he spits up on your suit jacket. You try your best to wipe it off but realize as you are back in your car that there is still a faint hint of white on your navy suit.

Your presentation is at 9:00 a.m. and you are supposed to meet with your boss and the entire team at 8:15 to review the final details. You're parking your car at 8:10 and know you are going to be late. Should you run to the bathroom to try to get this formula off of your coat or just go into the meeting and hope for the best?

You grab a wet paper towel on your way in and start dabbing your jacket. You apologize profusely for being late and try to quickly explain and laugh off the wardrobe issue that you are having. Some of the people in the room seem sympathetic. Your boss, clearly not amused, says, "I have repeatedly told you this is one of the most important meetings this company has ever had. The stakes are high and everything needs to be perfect. Please go clean yourself up and we will continue when you return."

You rush out to deal with your jacket and when you return you find that the meeting is nearly complete. Your boss gives you a stern glance and asks you to stay after while the rest of the group is dismissed, then says, "We need to get through this meeting and then you and I need to meet this afternoon to get a few things straight. Go set up your presentation and pick up your handouts. I will see you at the meeting."

You leave the room and think to yourself, "Geez . . . my boss is such _____."

How did you fill in the blank? Did you picture the boss as a man or a woman? If you pictured your boss as a man, take a moment and re-read the story picturing a female supervisor. If you pictured a woman, re-read with the boss as a male. Did you have a different reaction?

This case study is designed to make us think about the different ways that we expect leaders to act based on their gender. Let's picture the scenario with a different response from the boss, "Oh my, what a stressful morning you've had. I know that baby formula can be tough to get out of a suit. Last year, when Alyssa was a baby, I felt like I was coming to work with formula and baby food on my suit every day. Just take a minute and try to get that clean before the meeting." Do your thoughts or expectations about the gender of the boss change? Do your thoughts about the leadership capacities of the boss change?

Girls and women are in a dilemma. When they perform the behaviors that have been associated with effective leadership, they violate the conventions of appropriate female behavior and can be viewed as overly harsh or unfeminine (Catalyst, 2007). As one high school girl I interviewed said, "People get nervous if girls are too opinionated or direct. So if we stand up for ourselves, or are too strong, they will call you a bitch." Conversely, when girls and women do not engage in the more traditional leadership behaviors, they are often viewed as poor leaders. To solve this problem, one of two things could happen:

1. Girls need to learn to develop increased comfort with some of the traditional traits and characteristics that have been associated with effective leadership.

2. The way that we define and conceptualize leadership needs to change.

I believe that both of these things need to happen. Girls need to be comfortable speaking their mind, standing up for themselves, making a decision and taking responsibility for it, and taking initiative to create change. We also need to expand the definition and understanding of leadership to incorporate different approaches and a wide variety of skill sets.

A NEW MODEL OF LEADERSHIP

How can we construct a new model of leadership for girls? We need to focus on the actual skills, traits, and dispositions that we want girls to develop that will assist them in effectively navigating their lives while helping them develop a leadership identity. As we do this, we also need to work to promote the understanding that leadership takes on different forms and requires a wide range of skills, attitudes, and behaviors. The narrow definitions of leadership have served to limit girls' participation because they do not see their own skills as leadership skills.

We can draw on the research of several different organizations that focus on girls' leadership development to bring together the components necessary for fostering girls' leadership. Girl Scouts USA (2008), CARE USA (2009), and the Ms. Foundation (2000) have all publicized various works focusing on girls' leadership development. In the following section I summarize and extend their findings and recommendations:

- *Passion:* "I know what I care about."

Girls need opportunities to be exposed to many different people, places, issues, and ideas in order to determine what it is that they are passionate about. A leader has to believe in what she is doing in order for others to believe in it as well.

- *Motivation:* "I have identified something that I care about and I am willing to do something about it."

Girls can feel passionately about an issue, but they must also develop the motivation to take action. This demonstrates that they care enough to actually do something about it.

- *Creativity:* "I know what I am good at."

When girls identify a passion and the motivation to create change, they must determine how they are going to create the change. What are their individual skills and gifts? How can they most effectively use their energies in the most productive and useful ways?

- *Assertiveness:* "I am willing to stand up for myself and the topic/idea/principle/project that I care about."

Leaders must possess the ability to articulate their thoughts and make decisions. They should ask questions and be assertive because they believe that their opinions matter.

- *Decision Making:* "I know that the decisions that I make matter to me and to my community."

Leaders recognize that they often need to make difficult decisions and that sometimes their decisions impact others.

They recognize that they can create opportunities for themselves and the they are in control of their own decisions.

- ***Self-Confidence:*** "I like who I am and I value myself as a person. I can recognize my strengths and I know the things that I do well."

Leaders need to both possess and project confidence. They should recognize their internal value and worth and work to build up those around them.

- ***Organization and Follow Through:*** "I can see the project through from start to finish. I organize myself to achieve my goals."

Having the idea, motivation, and wherewithal to start an initiative is all for naught if it lacks organization and follow through. Leaders will stay motivated and organized to ensure that their vision is achieved.

- ***Vision/Ability to Motivate Others:*** "I can bring people together to use their own skills and talents to accomplish something."

Leaders must develop the ability to involve others in their vision so that they are not alone in their journey. Empowering others to identify their strengths and the ways that their skills can be used increases engagement and commitment.

Thinking about leadership in this way creates an opportunity for girls to see where they can fit into the model. They can assess their own attributes and determine how they can use their skills and abilities to make an impact. We also want girls to have a broad sense of what leadership looks like from the perspective of successful female leaders. What do they do and how do they describe themselves?

PREPARING GIRLS FOR LEADERSHIP

What do we want girls to accomplish by developing leadership skills? What do we want them to be doing differently after they participate in a leadership program? How can we prepare them for the challenges that they will face as they attempt to exercise their leadership capacities in different environments? These are the questions that I believe we need to explore as we consider building young female leaders.

Female Leaders Describe Their Leadership Styles

While it is important to look at the traits that help girls become leaders, it is also important to study flourishing female leaders to understand the attributes they possess and activities that they engage in that have helped them become successful leaders. Susan Madsen (2008) studied the leadership styles of women who are presidents of colleges and universities. These women described themselves in the following ways:

She is . . .		*She . . .*
A consensus builder	Ethical	Communicates well
A risk taker	Fair	Delegates
A strong communicator	Honest	Develops others
An analyzer	Nice	Does not micromanage
Business-minded	Not afraid	Engages others
Committed	Open to criticism	Gives credit to others for successes
Collaborative	Open to learning from mistakes	Has a deep understanding of the issues
Confident	Perceptive	Has a strong personality
Cooperative	Plain spoken	Has detailed knowledge
Decisive	Productive	Has high standards
Demanding of self	Results-focused	Has strength
Demanding of others	Supportive	Hires the best people
Focused	Team-oriented	Involves others in decision making
Inclusive	Service-oriented	Listens well
Engaging	Visionary	

I was part of a collaborative research project where we sought to understand the big things going on in girls' lives, as described by the girls themselves. We also wanted to know what girls would actually want to talk about if they were in a group that was just for girls. Girls' responses ranged from girl drama, to boys, to body image, to academics. We were surprised to see that leadership was one of the items that received the lowest endorsement from the girls. It was not one of the top things that girls said they wanted to talk about.

However, this does not mean that parents and educators should forgo their efforts to develop leadership among girls. Rather it means that we need to embed leadership development activities into other programming that is addressing the issues that are affecting girls. Often adults believe that leadership development is critical for youth; however, girls sometimes find that there are other issues that they are dealing with that feel more relevant to their present-day lives than leadership.

For girls who live very intense lives and are dealing with stressors such as living in violent homes or communities, attempting to get their basic needs met, dealing with dating or sexual violence, and dealing with the daily drama between and among girls, developing leadership seems to be of secondary importance to managing the challenges of day-to-day life. We, as adults, can recognize that developing leadership would help girls in all those areas, but we need to connect to the girls in the most relevant and accessible manner.

We also need to ensure that all girls have access to opportunities to enhance their skills and develop a leadership identity. Too often only a select group of girls have access to leadership development activities, programs, and training. Girls are often targeted at young ages for being confident or outgoing and are selected for leadership positions in their school, troops, or youth groups, while other girls who are less outgoing or charismatic get left behind.

WHAT CAN WE DO?

☆ Provide safe girl-only spaces for trying out new skills

Girls need the opportunity to have all-girl environments where they can explore new and different ways of being and relating to others. Building a space that is emotionally safe, confidential, and empowering allows girls to explore their thoughts and ideas, challenge their thinking or beliefs, and try out new behaviors. It is much easier to try out something new and scary if you are in a setting where you will be supported and reinforced. If you have to worry about your emotional safety, or that you are going to get made fun of or criticized, you are less likely to want to try anything new or take a risk.

☆ Connect girls with female leaders in your community

Strong female leaders can act as mentors and role models to girls and young women. Mentors can provide an authentic voice while giving honest feedback to girls. The truth is that leadership is not without its challenges, and many female leaders will tell you that they have had to sacrifice some things as they moved up the leadership ladder. Allowing girls to meet and talk with women from various backgrounds provides the opportunity for girls to become inspired—or not—by different experiences. I was working with a young women's leadership academy and was interviewing the participants after they completed an 18-month program. Throughout the experience, the young women had the opportunity to interact with a variety of female leaders from different backgrounds and disciplines. Some of the leaders were very high-powered executives who worked in very stressful but rewarding and influential jobs. The leaders talked about their rise to the top, their decisions to have or not have children, and the ways that they manage their business and their home life. They shared the challenges that they face as female executives in a male dominated arena and the difficulty that they have managing their time and getting everything done. As I interviewed the young women participants after their exposure to the women leaders, it was interesting to see that some became inspired and excited by their experience with these high-powered women. Others saw the difficult and demanding lifestyle and determined that they might not be a good fit for that type of leadership position. However, without the exposure they would not really know what they think or feel regarding various leadership options for women. Bringing guest speakers to your school or community organization or having girls interview or job shadow different types of women leaders are ways that girls can expand their leadership understanding and exposure.

☆ Teach teens that leadership skills are skills for success; they are not boys' skills or girls' skills

Despite the fact that some leadership characteristics and traits have been coded traditionally masculine or traditionally feminine, there are attributes of leadership that all girls would benefit by possessing. For example, assertiveness is generally a characteristic associated with boys and men; however, it is a skill that is also necessary for effective leadership. Assertiveness does not mean aggressiveness or demanding to get one's own way; rather, it means ensuring that your voice and opinions are offered. Being a good listener, demonstrating empathy, or creating an environment of mutual respect and collaboration are all traits of effective leadership. Yet these would also be characteristics that are more associated with a feminine approach to leadership. There are many skills associated with effective leadership and whether they are connected to boys or girls should be irrelevant; rather, we should focus on the skills and outcomes that we want girls to develop as they begin to develop a leadership identity. The reality is that all these skills are necessary for success as a leader.

☆ Allow girls to demonstrate leadership by giving them opportunities for meaningful participation

Girls need opportunities to demonstrate leadership both in and outside of the school setting. Parents, teachers, counselors, and administrators can intentionally provide opportunities for girls to develop their leadership skills while adding value to the school or home environment. For example, at home, give girls an opportunity to research and plan a family activity or trip. Invite girls to share their opinions and develop the skills to defend their perspectives. If your daughter does not think that a particular expectation or consequence that you have in place is fair, invite her to propose and present an alternative solution, and then together you can discuss the pros and cons. In schools, give girls opportunities to research and develop policies, spearhead extracurricular activities and initiatives, and help contribute in a positive manner to the school climate. One of the best examples I have seen of this is when a new charter school opened in my community. The school was still developing their policies on student behavior and school climate. A small group of high school girls were concerned that there was no student code or policy that addressed sexual harassment. They brought their concerns to the administration and instead of the school leadership drafting a policy and presenting it to the students, they empowered the girls to take the initiative to research and develop a model sexual harassment policy for the school. The students spent weeks conducting surveys, running focus groups, and hosting brainstorming sessions, until they developed and proposed a policy complete with examples, expectations of student behavior, reporting procedures, and consequences. The girls were able to have a leadership role in a process that had a substantial and systemic impact on their school and their educational experience.

☆ Remind girls that not everyone is going to like them, and that is okay

In general, girls feel great pressure to be nice, helpful, and caring. The helping aspects of leadership resonate with most girls more so than any other facet of leadership. The challenge to this is that girls also report a concern about not being liked if they were a leader. Girls feel pressure to choose between relationships and leadership (Girl Scouts Research Institute, 2008) and will work to ensure that the people around them are happy—sometimes at the expense of their own happiness. When girls stand up for themselves or participate in leadership activities, there is always the chance that their friends, family, and peers will not agree with them. Sometimes this fear is enough to keep girls from speaking up, making decisions, or having opinions that are different. We need to prepare girls for the reality that when they do speak up or assert their leadership, they may not be liked by everybody. This does not mean that they should stop these behaviors; rather it means that girls need to be emotionally ready for any negative fallout. Our job is to let them know that this is a possibility and a reality for all successful leaders and to equip them with the skills to effectively manage these situations and emotions.

CHAPTER 9

What Girls Want

*A*n authentic connection with girls and an understanding of their experiences is something that everyone who works with or cares about girls seeks to accomplish. Hundreds of parents and teachers in workshops, focus groups, and interviews openly express their concerns for the girls in their lives and their genuine desire to increase their communication and promote the girls' success. However, the more that we approach our work with girls by telling them what we think they need, the less relevant we become. Adults do have a great deal of insight into the needs of girls, yet they often fail to take the time to adequately listen to the girls in their lives. We need to approach our relationships with girls from a position of seeking to understand. We want to understand and connect with them so that we can keep the lines of communication open and we need to know, from girls, how to best accomplish this.

It has been interesting to realize that one of the top ways adults believed that they could connect best to girls was unfortunately one of the top things that girls said drive them crazy. Adults want girls to know that they have experienced similar things and will say to girls, "When I was your age . . ." and "I know how you feel, I had the same thing happen to me at your age." For adults, this initially seems that we are letting them know that we understand what they are going through, that we have had a similar experience, and that we can comprehend their feelings. We want to be contemporary and relevant while we communicate a sense of understanding. "I have been there—I know how this feels."

Intellectually, this makes sense because most of us were there and we do have some sense of how girls might be feeling. However, many teens have the perspective that no one can understand what they are feeling or going through—especially an adult. They truly believe that their situation is so unique that they may be the first person to ever feel what they are feeling at this particular moment. So when we say, "I know how you feel" it makes us seem even more out of touch (were that possible!) than we already are. We are adults—(yikes!) moms, dads, teachers, and so far removed from the intense realities of girls' lives (or so they think) that the thought that we could understand their feelings is so not cool.

This phenomenon is what human development researchers refer to as the *personal fable*. It is the idea that my experiences are completely unique and that no one else can possibly understand me—especially an adult (Vernon, 2009). This sense of isolation can play itself out in various ways in girls' lives and can distance them from their peers and from the caring adults in their lives. However, when we put girls in a space together and provide them with the opportunity to discuss the things going on in their lives, they are always surprised to learn that the other girls are going through the same things that they are going through. While this seems like common and logical sense to us, to the girls it truly feels revolutionary to find out that other girls are having similar experiences. They realize that other girls are having similar intense, confusing, and isolating thoughts and they don't feel so alone. They feel a sense of belonging and understanding.

Our goal should not be to convince girls that we have been there and that we do understand. Girls believe that their issues are far more serious than anything we could have experienced, and as such, to relate to us around their problems seems impossible. Our role as adults is not to make them see our perspective but rather we should seek to understand their current experience. This doesn't happen without listening and withholding judgment. Teens also tend to view adults as being "way older" and removed from their issues and also view parents' or teachers' experiences as being irrelevant to their lives. While many of the issues addressed in this book stand the test of time in regards to the problems that girls are dealing with, there are also many experiences and concerns that are, in fact, unique to today's girls and teens. Think about the issues surrounding technology and social media. Most of us did not have to deal with those issues as teenagers. Showing interest without having to be the expert is another way to demonstrate effective listening skills with girls.

WE ASKED GIRLS, "HOW CAN ADULTS BETTER SUPPORT YOU? WHAT DO YOU NEED FROM THE ADULTS IN YOUR LIFE?"

When we ask girls what they want from the adults in their lives many of the comments focused around issues of communication and trust. Overwhelmingly, girls feel that the adults in their lives do not trust them and that they do not have effective ways to communicate in positive and constructive ways with parents, teachers, and other adults in their lives. Adults feel quite similar, "I have no idea how to talk to these girls." They are frustrated by their inability to "get to" girls and they feel that girls are "impossible to talk to."

Clearly communication has broken down; however, there are strategies to help the situation, and I believe that it is the adults' responsibility to figure out new ways of communicating with and relating to teen girls. Girls say that they would rather talk to their peers or to girls who are older than them rather than adults. When we asked them why they don't want to talk to adults, they told us that adults don't get them, they don't understand, and that they don't really care. The reality is that many adults care very deeply about the girls in their lives; however, they lack the skills to adequately communicate this care and concern and then are unable to connect effectively with girls.

We asked the girls, "If the adults in your life could better support you, or if you could tell the adults in your life anything that you wanted about how to best support you, what would you tell them?" Not surprisingly, the things that girls said were amazingly consistent. Girls of all ages, races, and backgrounds had similar ideas about how the adults in their lives could best support and encourage them. I selected several of the most recurring themes to share with you in this chapter.

"LISTEN TO WHAT WE HAVE TO SAY. CONSIDER HOW WE FEEL AND JUST LISTEN INSTEAD OF JUMPING TO CONCLUSIONS."

Girls do not feel listened to. They feel that adults do not spend the time to listen to what they're actually saying, and when they do, girls feel that adults think their problems and feelings are stupid or childish. Girls talk about sharing certain concerns or feelings with adults, and then, instead of the adults affirming their feelings or the situation, the adults jumped to a conclusion and began to offer advice or tell the girl that how she handled the situation was wrong and that she needs to do something differently.

Often, we just want people to listen to what we have to say. We are not always looking for advice; we're not always looking for their opinion; we're just looking to be heard and to feel that we are understood. The same thing applies for girls; they just want to know that we are listening to them and that we are trying to understand the situation, as difficult as that might be for us.

Listen to understand. Don't listen to respond. This is perhaps one of the hardest concepts for any of us to comprehend. We become so accustomed to listening to what other people are telling us, that instead of truly trying to understand what they are saying and comprehend the actual feeling and meaning, we constantly try to think of what our response should be. We are thinking of what should come out of our mouth next, instead of taking the time to hear what is being said. How fantastic would it feel if we told someone a problem that we were dealing with and they simply said, "Wow, that is too bad . . . I'm so sorry that happened"? Unfortunately, we rarely respond like this. Rather, we try to think of the next response or the next thing that we should say. Girls need an adult who will just listen without judgment and without offering advice. Tina, a fifth grader, said, "Don't tell me that my feelings are stupid. I can't help how I feel." Even as adults we know that we need to be heard, valued, validated, and understood. We just want someone to tell us that we are okay and that our feelings are okay. Girls want the same thing. They just want us to listen, to care, and to let them know that what they are feeling or thinking is okay.

"STOP YELLING AND TALK MORE TO ME. YELLING AT ME ISN'T GOING TO MAKE THINGS BETTER."

Girls perceive that the adults in their lives are constantly yelling at them. They say they get yelled at by their teachers and by their parents and that when the yelling starts they simply "tune out" the person who is yelling. Adults say that they don't like to yell and that they wish they didn't have to yell. Many have stated that they do not yell until they have, "calmly asked several times for something to happen." Girls, however, feel that they are constantly being yelled at. Obviously there is a disconnect here because the perceptions of the parents and the girls are very different.

I know what happens to me when somebody yells at me. I get very adrenalized and yell back louder, or I retreat and completely tune out the other person. Obviously, neither of these strategies is effective in enhancing communication or accomplishing much of anything. As one seventh-grade girl shared, "Talk to me in a calm voice and I will understand you." We all want to be treated with dignity and respect. Yelling at one another makes us feel defensive, guarded, belittled, and demeaned. We need to calm ourselves down before we can expect to have a useful conversation. We can role model healthy and effective communication by interrupting the yelling exchange and saying, "Let's take a time-out from this conversation for a few hours and come back to it later when we are both cooled off."

"DON'T FREAK OUT WHEN I TELL YOU THINGS. WHEN YOU DO, IT MAKES ME WISH I NEVER TOLD YOU."

Girls sometimes want to share information with adults, but they will gauge what they share based on the reaction of the adults. If I know that you are going to start yelling at me if I tell you something, I am going to think twice before I tell you. We tell girls to share with us when they have difficult experiences, are upset by their peers, have had something bad happen to them or are angry or frustrated. Yet when they tell us some of these difficult things our own internal sense of protection kicks in. We get angry when there is injustice and protective when there is harm. Because we care so deeply for our girls, it can be difficult for us to keep our composure when we believe that our child or student has been taking advantage of, hurt, or mistreated.

Girls learn at young ages to observe the adults around them and to ensure that they don't do anything that will distress them further. This can mean that girls will restrict their own emotional responses if they sense that adults will get angry or sad. They don't want to be the cause of our distress, so they will restrict their emotions, only share limited information with us, or not tell us anything at all. As girls learn to read the emotions of the people around them, they also learn how to manage those emotions. Girls do not want to upset the people that they care about, and so it is often easier for them to keep things to themselves, rather than deal with the negative reactions of the adults that they may talk to.

For example, I was talking to an eleventh-grade girl, Shawna, who skipped school with one of her friends to meet up with some college guys. It was a Friday afternoon and the girls drove down to the university campus to meet up with the boys and their friends. The girls had been drinking some alcohol and throughout the course of the day Shawna and her friend got separated. When Shawna finally found her friend several hours later, she seemed out of it and was crying. As they drove home, Shawna's friend told her that two of the guys made her do stuff sexually that she didn't want to do. She said that she didn't know what to do or who she could talk to. I asked Shawna if she had talked to her parents or anybody at school about the situation. She laughed and said, "You're kidding, right? If I told anyone at school I'd get in trouble for skipping school. And if I even try to talk to my mom or dad about this, I can only imagine what I would hear. I bet they would care less about the fact that my friend was taken advantage of and more about the fact that I skipped school and was drinking. There is no way in the world that I would even think about telling them anything that happened."

While this is an extreme example, other girls have shared similar situations of intense responses from adults surrounding difficult situations that girls face. A seventh grader told me about a situation where she was being bullied on the bus every day by a group of ninth-grade girls. She said that the girls would make her leave the seat she was sitting in and go to another seat. When she would move to a different seat, then they would laugh and make her move seats again. She told me that this happened every day and that she didn't know what to do about it. She decided to tell her mom about what was happening. She said, "Then my mom went crazy. She was so mad at the ninth-grade girls and started to say things like, 'Who do they think they are telling people where they can and can't sit on the school bus? Do they own the school bus? I don't think so!' Then my mom said that she was going to come to the bus stop with me tomorrow and get on the bus and 'give those girls a piece of her mind.' I begged her not to do that; I can't imagine what would happen if she actually did that. It would be the worst thing ever, and I would never live that down. I know that I will think twice before I tell her anything like that again."

We are responsible for our own emotions and our responses. As adults, we have an increased ability to control our emotions and more sophisticated coping skills for managing anger or conflict. When girls feel like they have to sensor themselves so they can regulate our emotions, we are not providing them a safe place to share their thoughts or experiences, nor are we providing them with good role modeling for how they can handle tough situations.

"YOU JUST TELLING ME NOT TO DO SOMETHING IS GOING TO MAKE ME WANT TO DO IT MORE."

Adolescence is a time where girls seek to develop their own individual identities while they push the limits of adult authority. Girls seek to be independent but recognize that they also need and want caring adults in their lives. Girls can be curious and inquisitive and may want to try out new experiences and "live on the edge." They want to explore new things, new relationships, and want to be cool and accepted in their social circles. Have you ever heard, "But Janelle's parents are letting her go; I don't get what the big deal is. No one else's parents care. This is so not fair"?

Adults have a tremendous need to protect the girls in their lives and often try to restrict and limit their behaviors for their own well-being and safety. Unfortunately, girls can internalize these limits as perceived challenges. "If you are not going to let me do something, I am going to figure out a way to actually do it."

We are often drawn toward things that we perceive to be "off limits" and sometimes think, "If you tell me that I can't have it or can't do it, then I want to have it or do it even more." Developmentally, teenagers are right in that space. Pushing boundaries and limits is part of the adolescent experience.

Ninth grader Toni shared with me an experience about wanting to put blue colored streaks in her hair. She said that her entire field hockey team was going to put semipermanent blue dye streaks in their hair for their upcoming championship game. When Toni talked to her mother about it, she said her mom "totally freaked out." Her mom said, "Absolutely not. You will not dye your hair. That's absolutely ridiculous." Toni asked her mom why she thought it was so stupid, and her mom said, "You have beautiful hair, don't you dare do anything to ruin that." Toni told me, "It was like she was totally missing the point. To tell the truth, up until that point I didn't really want to do it. I thought it looked kind of stupid and I was secretly afraid that the blue would stay in my hair longer than I wanted it to. But as soon as my mom told me that I wasn't allowed to do it, I decided that I absolutely had to do it. So I figured out a way to stay at my friend's house that weekend so that we could both dye our hair together. My mom almost lost her mind when I came home that weekend. I thought it was really funny."

This is a more lighthearted example of how setting arbitrary limits can provoke an adolescent to push the boundaries and test the limits of authority. If the reaction of Toni's mother was more moderate and they had an opportunity to talk out the situation, perhaps the response would have been different. What if Toni's mom had said, "Wow . . . blue hair . . . Tell me what you think about that?" At that point, Toni wasn't really sold on the idea of dyeing her hair blue and probably would've said, "I'm not really sure about it, I think it looks kind of silly, but everybody else seems to be doing it." How different the reaction, and the ensuing response, may have been if this conversation had happened.

"ACCEPT US FOR WHO WE ARE AND DON'T PRESSURE US TO BE DIFFERENT."

Girls tell me that they feel intense pressure from teachers, parents, and their peers. The pressure can be related to how they look, what they're good at, who their friends are, and how they perform academically. Girls feel like they are often compared to others and that they don't always measure up.

"Don't compare me to my sister, or compare me to what you were doing at my age. Just compare me to me." Girls want to be valued and appreciated for who they individually are, not who they are in relation to other people. Girls don't want to feel like they have to live up to the achievements of their siblings or to their parents. They want to be successful and accomplished for themselves and not always feel like they have something to prove to others. "I just want them to think that I am good enough like I am. I don't want everyone to think that I have to change or be something different to be okay in their eyes."

Helping girls identify their own unique strengths, abilities, and skills can help them realize that their own special talents are important. If everything that a girl accomplishes is viewed in comparison to her siblings, her classmates, or her teammates, then she may constantly be trying to keep up with or compete with someone else. This message tells her that she, herself, is just not good enough but rather she has to be better than everyone else to be okay in our eyes.

> *"I feel so much pressure to be perfect. I have to get perfect grades, do perfect in sports, and even look perfect. I have to get into a good college and I need to get an athletic or academic scholarship to be able to pay for it. I feel like if I mess one thing up that I am letting everyone down and disappointing my parents or my teachers. I hear my parents talk to other parents, and I realize that they are so proud of me . . . but that makes me feel even more pressure. I have to do well so that my parents aren't embarrassed of me! There is nothing worse than hearing someone say that they are disappointed in you. I can deal with them being mad at me but disappointed in me is totally different."* —Jaylee, eleventh grade

Girls internalize the expectations that are communicated to them and, while we want to hold high expectations for girls, we need to be mindful of the ways that girls may experience pressure. As adults it is easy to look at the lives of middle or high school students and yearn for those carefree days! As we look back, we think that we didn't have to worry about a thing—no mortgage or health insurance to worry about, no kids to take care of, no bills to pay. So what could a teen actually have to worry about? In their minds, plenty.

The stress that teens feel is real. Their lives are full of things that legitimately stress them out. As Jaylee stated above, she feels that she is dealing with a lot of big issues and decisions. Comparing her issues to our adult issues only serves to minimize her experience and her feelings. Lindsee, an eighth grader said, "I was telling my dad that I was so stressed out trying to get good grades so that I could get into a good high school. He totally laughed at me and said that there was no way I could be stressed out. He said that I needed to wait until I had a job and a house and a family and then I would know what stress feels like." How different would Lindsee have felt if her dad had said, "Honey, tell me what is stressing you out"?

"DON'T BE UP IN OUR BUSINESS ALL THE TIME. WE NEED SOME PRIVACY AND YOU NEED TO TRUST US MORE."

Girls desperately feel a need for privacy that generally begins around puberty and gets more intense as they progress through early and midadolescence. Girls are trying to make sense of what is happening to their bodies while they are trying to navigate relationships with friends. They want to figure things out on their own and may be unlikely to feel that adults have much to offer in the way of guidance around these issues. Girls report having parents and teachers that are always "in their business" and are always trying to get information about where they are, who they're with, and what they're doing.

While adults recognize that this is part of monitoring teens and ensuring that they are doing the right things, girls see it as restrictive and intrusive. "Sometimes I feel like adults always think that we're up to no good. That everything that we are doing is wrong or sneaky and that we're always doing something to get into trouble. Sometimes we just need time with other people our age, and we don't want adults to be around. There are lots of things that we can't talk about with our parents or our teachers, so we just need time to talk to our friends about some things."

I have a friend whose mother is, like, totally in her business all the time. It's like she can't even make a phone call without her mom knowing who she is calling. Her mom goes online and prints out the phone numbers that she calls and texts that she sends and she goes over them with her every month. She's not allowed to have a lock on her bedroom door, and her mom just comes in and goes through her stuff whenever she wants. Every time I'm over there her mom always asks me all kinds of questions about our friends, and I sometimes feel nervous about talking to her. I know that my friend doesn't tell her mom very much anymore. She feels like everything that she talks about she's going to get in trouble for, so she figures she'll just leave lots of details out. Like last week we were going to the mall and meeting up with some friends, but she told her mom that it was just the two of us going. I think sometimes it's easier to just leave information out, than have to deal with getting in trouble. I guess it would be different if we were actually doing something to get in trouble, but we're not. I just don't get why parents don't trust teenagers at all. It's not even like we've done anything to make them not trust us, they just don't, and it doesn't seem like there's anything that we can do about it.

It can be hard for adults to trust teenagers, particularly when the adults were all teenagers once and know what they did during their teenage years. Some parents have said to me, "I know that I couldn't talk to my mom and dad growing up, and I don't want the same thing to happen for my daughter." Unfortunately, it seems that most teenage girls don't feel like their parents trust them and don't feel like they can talk to them about serious issues. Talking openly about issues of trust and how trust and respect are gained and lost is an important conversation that, unfortunately, does not happen with great frequency. Helping girls understand how they demonstrate that they are trustworthy and respectful and treating them with the appropriate levels of trust and respect are important for maintaining an open and communicative relationship. When they perceive that the default position is that they are not trustworthy and that they are not respected, then girls will retreat from the relationship and view it as more adversarial than supportive.

GIRLS WANT TO BE TAKEN SERIOUSLY

Too often adults think that girls' concerns and problems are immature and juvenile; however, to girls the issues that they're dealing with are serious and stressful. As we try to understand the way that girls are processing their experiences, we have to take into consideration their chronological and developmental level. The adolescent brain is still developing, and girls' cognitive complexity is limited. Sometimes when we hear the issues that girls say are impacting their lives and the issues that they believe to be important, it is hard for us, as adults, to see them as legitimate concerns.

We easily question how girls can get so upset about things that seem silly or inconsequential. There are a couple reasons for this: (1) Adolescents are not able to process information and experiences in the same way that adults can, and (2) adolescents have not had the experiences, or frame of reference, that adults have to manage emotional situations.

When girls are upset about friendships, dating, or school and we minimize their concerns, it reinforces to them that we don't understand their reality. Girls want their concerns to be taken seriously. When we listen to them express their concerns, we have to remember that we are looking at the situation from *our* view. This view probably includes many more years, many more friendships and relationships, and much more life experience. Our view also includes a fully developed brain and a much more sophisticated and cognitively complex way of thinking and reasoning. Part of how girls are making sense of their situation is based on their biology—or their inability to think in abstract ways—as well as their experience and frame of reference. When we hear things that sound silly, unbelievable, or just plain immature, we have to remember that girls see the situation as serious and meaningful. Despite what we might be feeling or thinking on the inside, we must communicate care and concern to girls to show that we are seeking to understand their reality and what is happening to them at this very moment.

All these identified themes lead to breakdowns in communication among adolescents and adults and, as we know, communication is crucial in any relationship, especially when trying to help the girls in our lives. Just as discussed in previous chapters on girls' relationships with other girls, many girls do not come back to relationships with their parents until much later in life, if at all. They simply find other individuals who seem to have an open mind about their experiences and who listen to them without judgment when sharing their problems. Girls are not looking for friendships with the adults in their lives. They don't want their parents or their teachers to be their "best friends," but they do want these people to understand, believe, and respect them.

It is important to understand that it is *okay* if our daughters don't tell us *everything* that is going on in their lives at this very moment. Chances are, when they are ready, they will tell us what they need us to know about the tough situations in their lives, but we need to give them the space to do so. We demonstrate our understanding and respect for girls by taking the time to listen to what they're saying, connect with them in meaningful ways, and support them through their difficult challenges. When we give girls the ideal balance of space, privacy, trust, and respect, they tend to give the same balance back to adults.

CHAPTER 10

What Girls Need

GIRLS NEED TO BE THE EXPERTS ON THEIR OWN LIVES

When we allow girls to be the experts on their own lives, we work to intentionally place them in a position of knowing. This means that when we talk to girls we allow them to describe their experiences, their thoughts, and their perspectives to us rather than telling them what these perspectives should be. In counseling, we call this taking a "one-down" position. It means that we purposefully and intentionally approach the relationship or the conversation from a position of not knowing and allow ourselves to give up some power to allow the other person to perceive that they have some control in the relationship (Vernon, 2009).

When adults and teenagers interact, there is always an inherent power differential. In almost every situation, an adult has more power than a teenager. I am not talking about physical power but rather age, societal, and interpersonal factors that can play into the dynamics of any relationship. There are many relationships that have an inherent power differential: teacher-student, principal-teacher, boss-employee, and parent-child. If we want to create environments and opportunities for others to feel safe and valued, we need to take an active role in mitigating that power differential.

This can start by simply deciding where we sit when we are talking to young girls. Do we stand over their desks while we ask them to explain themselves, or do we sit down next to them at a chair or a desk of the same height? Do we sit behind our giant and intimidating desk in our big leather executive chair, or do we plop down on the floor and ensure that we are at the same relative height as the student? Physical proximity and physical placement has a lot to do with how people perceive power dynamics and authority. So part of taking this one-down position is placing yourself alongside the girl that you're talking to. When we do this, we communicate to the girl that we are here, alongside her, and we are coming at the conversation from a place of equality rather than superiority.

Another aspect of taking a one-down position is to come at the conversation from a "not knowing" position. This means that we allow the girl to be the expert on her life and describe it to us. We seek to understand her reality by asking her to teach us about it. We might say things such as, "Help me understand how this argument with your friend really feels," or "I don't really know much about field hockey, maybe you can teach me more about it," or "I don't think I have a lot of information on the kind of social media that teenagers are using these days, tell me some of the things that kids at your school are using." Taking a one-down position is an intentional communication strategy that shifts the power dynamic in a relationship and provides the opportunity to allow the teenager to be the expert on their life and perhaps even the expert in the conversation. It is an effective strategy for beginning to build rapport and provides a sense of safety and comfort to the girl.

GIRLS NEED ADULTS TO COMMUNICATE OPENLY

I was talking with a mother who is very concerned about the changing dynamics of her relationship with her 13-year-old daughter. She says that they've always had an open and communicative relationship, however, lately things feel like they're changing. She says she has a hard time talking to her daughter, and every time she asks questions her daughter will give simple yes or no responses and then won't say more. I asked her to share with me a little bit about some of the questions that she asks her daughter. The mom said, "Every day when she comes home from school I ask her if she had a good day at school. My daughter will simply say 'Yeah, it was fine.' and that will be the end of the conversation. I feel like I'm just not getting the same kind of conversation that I used to get, even last year. Another example would be when my daughter comes home from a softball game and I know that they have won the game. I'll ask her, 'Hey honey how did the game go?' Depending on her mood she'll say, "It was good" or "It was fine," and then that feels like the end of the conversation."

Often closed questions such as these can lead to closed responses. For example, "Did you have a good day today?" can elicit a response that is "yes" or "no." If we rephrase that question and instead say, "Tell me about your day," we create the opportunity to have a very different conversation. Granted the response could be, "What do you want to know?" but it is more likely that this simple change in communication can open the lines of discussion even further. If "Did you have a good game?" was changed to "Tell me all about the game," we provide a different opening to have a different kind of conversation.

Using open-ended questions is an effective communication strategy with teenagers and adults alike. It demonstrates that we are interested in what the other person has to say, and it gives them the option to decide what is important or what they want to share with us. Even a simple, "Tell me about yourself" can elicit a disclosure from that person's own space. It allows them to decide what is important, what they want to tell us, and how they will share that with us. It can change the dynamic from a question-answer session to a more open, engaging, and rich conversation.

GIRLS NEED OPPORTUNITIES TO IMPROVE THEIR CONFIDENCE, SELF-ESTEEM, AND SELF-EFFICACY

In a survey I conducted with teachers, I asked them what they thought girls needed in order to be successful. Without fail, the number one response that teachers gave was that girls need more self-confidence. We know that self-esteem and self-confidence are related to almost every other dimension of our lives. Self-concept is connected to our academic achievement, our career development, our friendships and relationships, and our leadership development. If we have a strong sense of ourselves, know what we are good at, and have confidence in our abilities, then we are more likely to try new things, take risks, and put ourselves out there in a way that we may not if we were constantly doubting or questioning ourselves.

A strong sense of self is not something that we are born with; it develops based on our learnings and our interactions with others and our environment. If we have opportunities to explore and develop our skills, we are able to identify dimensions of ourselves that are strong and efficacious (Baldwin & Hoffman, 2002).

We want girls to have a positive *self-concept*, or *self-esteem*. These terms are generally interchangeable. They refer to the way that we feel about ourselves and the regard that we have for ourselves. Self-esteem develops through our childhood years and unfortunately drops during our adolescent years. The drop in self-esteem is greater for girls than it is for boys, and for many girls their self-esteem does not rebound after they progress through adolescence.

Another important term that is related to the way that we feel about ourselves is the term *self-efficacy*. Self-efficacy is different from self-esteem or self-concept in that it is related to my perception of myself as competent in different areas. Whereas self-concept is related to how I feel about who I am, self-efficacy is related to what I think I can do. It is my sense of myself as capable and my perception of my ability to do something well.

Our goal should be to enhance both the self-esteem and the self-efficacy of girls, and we do this by providing girls opportunities where they experience themselves being successful; where they can build their confidence and become more willing to try new things in the future.

We do not build self-esteem in girls by telling them that they are smart and pretty. Despite what we see in lots of girls' self-esteem programming, merely telling girls that they are beautiful or smart does not impact the way that they actually experience themselves. Building a stronger sense of self means that we believe that our value is internally derived. We have to actually feel it for ourselves and believe it about ourselves.

When I talk about enhancing girls' self-esteem, I always ask, "If I am not there every day to tell you that you are smart and beautiful and competent, do you experience yourself that way?"

Our sense of ourselves has to come from our internal experience, not from another's perception of us. While we are certainly subject to external pressures and influences, there is much that we can do to build the internal strength and fortitude of girls. A middle school teacher shared the following story with me:

I have a student, Lauren, in my eighth-grade class who is very shy but very smart. She gets great grades and is truly a self-regulated learner, but I feel like she lacks self-confidence. I notice that every time we do small group activities as a class, she is never the leader or the spokesperson for her group, although I am fairly confident that she has done the bulk of the work for her group. It is almost like she gets lost in the class because she's not sure of herself. I think she has so much potential, but I feel like her lack of confidence could hold her back. I have a great relationship with her and so I wanted my classroom to be a safe place for her to 'break out of her shell.' I started out by ensuring that I intentionally called on her when I knew she had the correct answer to a question. For example, after an exam, the students get their tests back and we review them as a class. Lauren generally does well on the exams, so I took note of her tests and what her strongest answers were, then in the review I made sure that she was called on to share at least one or two answers. She never volunteers on her own but is okay when she is called on. This gave her the opportunity to share in front of the class and gave me the opportunity to publicly praise her accomplishments. I noticed that after a couple weeks of doing this, she began to raise her hand to volunteer when she had the correct answer. I must admit I was really excited when I began to see these small changes in her confidence! We moved on from there to speaking in front of the class and eventually to taking the lead in a small group project. She rose to the occasion each time. It was like each time she realized that she could do it, she got more confident in her ability to actually do it.

We have to provide girls with opportunities to do things well. The "things" can be almost anything: communicating with friends, public speaking, making a campfire, shooting a basketball, changing a tire, standing up for themselves, sewing a button, cutting the grass, doing the dishes, completing a math equation, writing a poem, saying "no" to someone, competing in a science fair, or trying out for the choir. The vast opportunities that we provide girls to allow them to develop a new set of skills and competencies are the ways that we build their self-esteem, self-concept, and self-efficacy. Every opportunity that they engage in is an opportunity to build a set of skills.

Girls need to experience themselves as good at a lot of things, and unfortunately, many do not. Next time you are with a girl, ask her to name five things that she is good at. You will be surprised to see that some girls can give you a list of ten things, and some have trouble coming up with one. In fact, by the time girls get to high school, less than 30 percent would say that they are good at a lot of things. Girls need to find value in themselves that is not related to how they look but rather is related to who they are and what they're good at.

GIRLS NEED EXPOSURE TO REALISTIC AND POSITIVE FEMALE ROLE MODELS

"Girls just don't have anyone that they can look up to these days." I hear this from lots of adults who complain that there are no good role models for girls. In part, I can see how this is true. The images that girls see of women in the media are not overwhelmingly positive. Girls see many more images of women who are overtly sexual, lack career ambition, appear to be money or power-hungry, or are abusing drugs and alcohol than they see of strong, powerful, and competent women. One father told me, "I can't stand reality television. There's nothing positive on TV these days for my daughter to watch. All I see are shows that glorify things like teenage pregnancy, partying and hooking up, and cat fighting. I think it can make girls feel like there is something wrong with them if they *don't* have some kind of crazy problem. These are not the kind of influences that I want to expose my daughter to, but it seems like that is all that is out there right now—teen moms, really? Where are the strong role models and the positive influences? When do girls get to see images of people's lives that aren't so horrible? Where are the women that we want our girls to grow up to be like? I just am not seeing that anywhere."

He's right, there are not a large number of strong female role models on television right now and as we discussed earlier, the media influences on girls are extensive. We may be able to identify a few here and there; however, we need to expand our thinking of what a role model actually is. Role models do not need to be famous people, athletes, actresses, and movie stars. Role models can be regular people who do things well and that we admire. Our family members, teachers, coaches, and mentors can be role models. Arguably, the exposure to these "real life" role models has a more substantial impact on a girl's ability to see herself in a particular role than does the exposure to television stars or famous people who are seemingly out of her reach.

Girls need role models who look like them. They need to be exposed to women who may have had a similar background or experience and who is someone that they can relate to. Girls need to see people in a wide variety of jobs and careers. They need to see real women who get along with one another and support each other. They need to meet actual ladies who are athletes, community activists, businesswomen, and entrepreneurs. We need to broaden girls' horizons around what women *can* do and what women *actually* do. We want to give girls exposure to more of everything. More options, more occupations, more subjects, more culture, and overall more opportunity.

Where will we find these role models? Role models are women in our everyday lives. They are our colleagues, neighbors, friends, and associates. They are the people that have qualities and attributes that we want to emulate. A role model can be the neighbor girl next door who just got accepted into medical school. These women may not be perfect, but they have characteristics that are worthwhile and valuable for our girls to experience. In our research, we asked girls to identify who their role models are and tell us why they selected a particular person. The girls' responses ranged from famous musicians to actresses to teachers to family members. Interestingly, more than any other response, girls identified their mothers as their primary role model. Girls see traits in their mothers that they want to develop for themselves, such as strength, the ability to multitask, caring, self-sufficiency, and reliability. We all know lots of women who have these kinds of characteristics.

GIRLS NEED SPECIFIC PRAISE AND CONSTRUCTIVE REINFORCEMENT

Girls need positive reinforcement and encouragement. They need to feel that someone is supporting them and cares about them. Reinforcement for girls has often taken the shape of complimenting girls on their clothes, hair, or figure. In general, girls receive more compliments about how they look than they receive about what they do. As we work to shift this reality and focus our attention to the things that girls actually do well, we must ensure that our praise and reinforcement have the greatest impact.

Adults are eager to build up girls' self-confidence and self-esteem through providing them with positive reinforcement for being good, looking nice, and treating other people with respect. This type of praise—ongoing and general—does not actually have the impact on children that we would hope. When we reinforce kids for just "being great," we don't actually prepare them to do anything better. We actually prepare them instead to expect to receive ongoing praise for being great. Simply stated, ongoing general praise, and consistent messages about how great or wonderful you are, do little for improving how you feel about yourself. Instead you become accustomed to everyone telling you how wonderful you are and when you don't have that, you get upset (Bronson & Merryman, 2009).

When it comes to building self-esteem in an individual, what is most important is a person's internal sense of themselves. If our reinforcement comes from others' perceptions of our being "good enough," what happens when we don't have that?

We need to praise girls for their *effort* versus praising them for being smart. Kids who think they are just generally smart often will not put out as much effort as kids who believe that their effort is connected to their achievement. The kids who become so used to receiving praise learn to seek praise from adults and will actually take on fewer challenges because they are afraid to fail, afraid they won't receive praise, or afraid that they won't be labeled as "smart" (Bronson & Merryman, 2009).

This is not to suggest, by any means, that girls should not be praised and reinforced for the things that they do. Rather, we want to ensure that we are providing them with *quality* compliments and praise. Praise needs to be specific and sincere and provide the reinforcement that will have the greatest impact on her perception, her performance, and her persistence.

GIRLS NEED US TO BELIEVE THEM WHEN THEY TELL US THINGS THAT WE MAY NOT WANT TO BELIEVE

Sometimes girls have a difficult time sharing things with adults because they are afraid that they won't be believed. Particularly if the issue is related to another adult, girls assume that we will always take the side of the other adult. Their experience also supports this idea. Often when teenagers complain about a parent, teacher, or a coach the response back to them from other adults is generally, "Well, what did you do wrong to deserve that?" When girls feel like something is not fair, or that they've been mistreated, and they share their concerns with us, we must be mindful of how we respond.

I was working with a tenth-grade girl, Emily, who shared with me her experience of sexual inappropriateness on the part of her brother's friend. She talked about him making comments about her body and also trying to touch her breasts and buttocks when he was hanging out with her brother. She said that this went on for several weeks, and she kept telling him to stop. She told her brother also that this happened and he just laughed it off and said, "Shut up, you probably like it." She finally decided to tell her parents what was happening, and their response was "Emily, it's really hard to believe that he would do that. He's such a nice kid, and he comes from such a good family. We've never seen him do anything like that before; it feels pretty far-fetched."

Emily was devastated after talking with her parents. She felt like she was not believed, and her parents made her feel that she was lying about the situation. Why would she lie about something so serious? Unfortunately, when it comes to issues of sexual boundary crossings and child sexual abuse, children are likely to tell several adults before somebody actually believes their story. Girls need to know that we believe them and that we will protect them.

GIRLS NEED US TO TAKE THEIR CONCERNS SERIOUSLY AND NOT MINIMIZE THEIR EXPERIENCES

As mentioned before, girls are extremely frustrated and dismayed when adults do not take them seriously. Often, girls feel that their voices are unimportant, their opinions are devalued, and their contributions go unnoticed. We want to instill in girls at an early age that what they have to contribute is valuable and that we are interested in who they are and what they think. We want girls to know that we understand that their lives are intense and we respect their feelings. We may not be able to fully understand their feelings, but we have to respect how they feel.

Marcia shared a story with me about feeling like nobody really understood what was going on for her. Here's what she told me,

I have been really good friends with this one girl for about three years. When we started high school, she became very different. She started to hang out with a different group of kids and it seemed to me that our friendship was not as important to her as it used to be. We slowly started drifting apart, except that I kept trying to keep our friendship going. I would make plans to invite her to do things, I would get tickets for concerts and movies, and I would generally just look for opportunities for us to hang out. She would say things like, "Oh okay, that's cool; let's do that." But then she wouldn't show up when it was time to go somewhere. I actually had to go to a concert by myself because she ditched me. This sort of stuff went on for about six months and every time it happened my feelings would get really hurt. I kept a lot of it from my parents, because I figured that everything would get smoothed out soon enough and I didn't want them to hold a grudge against her. But the day that she embarrassed me at school was like the hardest day ever. She totally called me out in front of a whole group of students and then laughed at me in front of, like, the whole cafeteria. I was talking to my mom about what happened, and she said to me, "I've been watching what's been happening with her for months and I don't even know why you try to be friends with her. She's obviously not a very good friend, so why don't you just stop trying. You'll make new friends. You should just write her off now before she keeps hurting you." You know, I get what my mom is saying, but it just didn't feel good to hear it from her. It made me feel like she had no idea what I was feeling and no sense of how much I was hurting. I just wanted her to understand that everything sucks, and I don't need her to fix it, I just need her to get it.

Adults can also minimize the importance of puberty and periods in the lives of young girls. It is a really big deal when you are in the fourth, fifth, or sixth grade if you've gotten your period . . . or if you're the only one who *hasn't* gotten her period. Adults approach girls with a casual discomfort and air of humor and make comments about her "becoming a woman." Let's face it; no girl wants to hear that comment. We need to be sensitive to the fact that puberty is a really big deal. What your body looks like, what your hair looks like, and what your face looks like are all changing. We, as adults, have a hard time remembering the intensity of that experience. Instead of laughing it off when girls get their periods or have questions or concerns about what's happening to them, we need to provide them with support and good information.

Riley, a sixth-grade girl, talked about her experience talking to her mother about the fact that she had not yet gotten her period.

I remember talking to my mom after I got home from a sleepover at my friend's house. There were three other girls there and all of them had gotten their period last year except me. I wondered if something was wrong with me because they were all in the same grade as me and I was the only one left. I remember asking my mom a question about it and she said, "You should be glad you haven't gotten your period yet; it's such a pain; you're going to hate it anyway." I think I wasn't just concerned about getting my period, but my friends also have boobs and look way more grown-up than I do. I feel like I look like a baby next to my friends, but I couldn't really tell my mom that. I felt stupid for even bringing it up.

GIRLS NEED HELP IN LEARNING HOW TO ESTABLISH HEALTHY BOUNDARIES

There are many aspects of a girl's life where she needs to learn how to set boundaries and communicate those boundaries to others. We want girls to have control over their own experiences, bodies, relationships, academics, and careers. We want girls to believe that they have the right and the ability to stand up for themselves, their values, and their bodies if they don't agree with something or they feel that they are being taken advantage of.

One of the hardest things about defining boundaries and communicating them means that you're telling somebody else "No," or telling them something that they don't want to hear. This can be very difficult for girls and adults alike. Establishing boundaries means that you are setting guidelines around how you are willing to be treated by others and what access you allow other people in the world to have to you. Healthy boundaries mean that we, ourselves, get to decide what is okay with us and what is not. We put some insulation between us and the world in order to keep ourselves safe.

Defining boundaries can be difficult for girls, and in many ways, girls lack adequate role models of healthy and appropriate boundaries from the adults in their lives. I think about the impact of social media and how that has created blurred boundaries for many of us. Once, what we were thinking, wearing, eating, and even where we were, was our personal information that perhaps only a few people knew. Now, everyone in our "friend" network has lots of information about what we are doing at any given time. How do we tell girls to set boundaries around information that they share with others when, as adults, we are not doing a very good job of that ourselves?

Girls also need to learn how to establish boundaries around their body and dating. Girls need conversations about what is okay and what is not okay with them when it comes to dating. Girls need opportunities to practice verbalizing their boundaries before they find themselves in situations where they need to impose these limits.

GIRLS NEED HOPE FOR THE FUTURE

Finally, girls need hope for their futures and to know that we believe in them. We want to help girls see beyond their current circumstances or situations, no matter how difficult, and envision a rich and fulfilling life for themselves. We know that girls' experiences can be very different, and their lives can be full of difficulty and chaos, but girls are very resilient and possess the internal fortitude to rise above the situations where they find themselves to ultimately construct a life that they love.

Girls need to know that they can be anything that they want to be, but we have to support them to achieve these goals and prepare them for what they might face in their journey to realize their aspirations. We want girls to have access to the widest range of possibilities and options for their lives. We want girls to love being girls, not because they can wear dresses and get their hair done but rather because being a girl means that they can be anything they want to be, do anything they want to do, and go anywhere they want to go. We want them to understand that being a girl does not mean that you're limited in any way but rather that you are full of possibilities. Our role is to help girls see their own potential and to help them see the strength in themselves that they have difficulty identifying. We want girls to find value in themselves, so they can add value to the world.

Further Reading and Resources

SELF-ESTEEM/CONFIDENCE

- Deak, J., & Barker, T. (2002). *Girls will be girls: Raising confident and courageous girls.* New York, NY: Hyperion.

- Lloyd, G. (Ed.). (2005). *Problem girls: Understanding and supporting troubled and troublesome girls and young women.* London, UK: RoutledgeFalmer.

- Storm, H., & Jenkins, M. (2002). *Go girl! Raising healthy, confident and successful girls through sports.* Naperville, IL: Sourcebooks.

BODY IMAGE

- Chadwick, D. (2009). *You'd be so pretty if . . . : Teaching our daughters to love their bodies—even when we don't love our own.* Cambridge, MA: De Capo Press.

- Kilbourne, J., Jhally, S., & Media Education Foundation. (2010). *Killing us softly 4: Advertising's image of women.* Northampton, MA: Media Education Foundation.

- Newsom, J. S. (Director). (2011). *Miss representation.* [Documentary]. Sausalito, CA: Ro*co Films Educational.

CAREER DEVELOPMENT

- Cool Careers for Girls Series. (1999–2004). Set of 11 Books. Manassas Park, VA: Impact Publications. Available at www .impactpublications.com

- Savickas, M., & Hartung, P. J. (2012). *My career story: An autobiographical workbook for life-career success.* Available at http://www.vocopher.com/CSI/CCI_workbook.pdf

- Occupational Information Network (O*Net) at www.one tonline.org

ISSUES IN CYBERSPACE

- Bauman, S. (2011). *Cyberbullying: What counselors need to know.* Alexandria, VA: American Counseling Association.

- Childnet International. (2005–2012). *Digizen.* Retrieved from http://www.digizen.org

- Common Sense Media, Inc. (2012). *Common sense media.* Retrieved from http://www.commonsensemedia.org/

- Hinduja, S., & Patchin, J. (2008). *Bullying beyond the school yard: Preventing and responding to cyberbullying.* Thousand Oaks, CA: Corwin.

- Hinduja, S., & Patchin, J. (2012). *Cyberbullying research center.* Retrieved from http://www.cyberbullying.us/

- Willard, N. E. (2007). *Cyber-safe kids, cyber-savvy teens: Helping young people learn to use the internet safely and responsibly.* San Francisco, CA: Jossey-Bass.

GIRL PROGRAMS

- Girls' Circle Association at www.girlscircle.com

- Girls, Inc. at www.girlsinc.org

- Girls on the Run at www.girlsontherun.org

- Girl Scouts of the USA at www.girlscouts.org
- Ruling Our eXperiences, Inc. (ROX) at www.rulingour experiences.com

LEADERSHIP

- Catalyst. (2007). *The double-bind dilemma for women in leadership: Damned if you do, doomed if you don't.* New York, NY: Catalyst.
- Girl Scouts of the USA. (2008). *Change it up! What girls say about redefining leadership.* Girl Scout Research Institute, New York: NY.
- Gender and Empowerment Unit, CARE USA. (2009). *Girls' leadership development: Lessons from the field.* Atlanta, GA: Author.

RELATIONAL AGGRESSION

- Brown, L. M. (1998). *Raising their voices: The politics of girls' anger.* Cambridge, MA: Harvard University Press.
- Burton, B. (2009). *Girls against girls: Why we are mean to each other and how we can change it.* San Francisco, CA: Zest Books.
- Hirsch, L., Lowen, C., & Santorelli, D. (Eds.). (2012). *Bully: An action plan for teachers, parents, and communities to combat the bullying crisis.* New York, NY: Weinstein.
- Simmons, R. (2002). *Odd girl out: The hidden culture of aggression in girls.* New York, NY: Harcourt, Inc.

SEXUAL VIOLENCE/VIOLENCE

- American Psychological Association, Task Force on the Sexualization of Girls. (2010). *Report of the APA Task Force on the Sexualization of Girls.* Retrieved from http://www.apa.org/pi/women/programs/girls/report-full.pdf
- Chesney-Lind, M., & Jones, N. (Eds.). (2010). *Fighting for girls: New perspectives on gender and violence.* Albany, NY: SUNY Press.

- Joyful Heart Foundation at www.joyfulheartfoundation.org
- Rape, Abuse, and Incest National Network at www.rainn.org

FEMININITY/GENDER

- Barnett, R., & Rivers, C. (2004). *Same difference: How gender myths are hurting our relationships, our children, and our jobs.* New York, NY: Basic Books.
- Bennetts, L. (2007). *The feminine mistake: Are we giving up too much?* New York, NY: Hyperion.

PARENTING

- American Girl, LLC. (2009). *Raising an American girl: Parenting advice for the real world.* Middleton, WI: American Girl Publishing.
- Bronson, P., & Merryman, A. (2009). *NurtureShock: New thinking about children.* New York, NY: Hachette Book Group.
- Honoré, C. (2008). *Under pressure: Rescuing our children from the culture of hyper-parenting.* New York, NY: Harper One.
- Forsyth, S., & Ms. Foundation for Women. (1998). *Girls seen and heard: 52 life lessons for our daughters.* New York, NY: Tarcher/ Putnam.
- Tannen, D. (2006). *You're wearing that?: Understanding mothers and daughters in conversation.* New York, NY: Random House.
- Thompson, M., & Barker, T. (2004). *The pressured child: Helping your child find success in school and life.* New York, NY: Ballantine Books.
- Wiseman, R., & Rapoport, E. (2006). *Queen bee moms & king-pin dads: Dealing with parents, teachers, coaches, and counselors who make—or break—your child's future.* New York, NY: Crown Publishers.

References

American Association of University Women Educational Foundation. (2008). *Where the girls are: The facts about gender equity in education.* Washington, DC: Author.

American Association of University Women Educational Foundation. (2010). *Why so few? Women in science, technology, engineering, and mathematics.* Washington, DC: Author.

American Psychological Association, Task Force on the Sexualization of Girls. (2010). *Report of the APA Task Force on the Sexualization of Girls.* Retrieved from http://www.apa.org/pi/women/programs/girls/report-full.pdf

Armitage, C. (2012). Evidence that self-affirmation reduces body dissatisfaction by basing self-esteem on domains other than body weight and shape. *Journal of Child Psychology and Psychiatry, 53*(1), 81–88.

Baldwin, S. A., & Hoffmann, J. P. (2002). The dynamics of self-esteem: a growth-curve analysis. *Journal of Youth Adolescence, 31*(2), 101–113.

Bernard, B. (1993). Fostering resiliency in kids. *Educational Leadership, 51,* 44–48.

Biro, F. M., Striegel-Moore, R. H., & Franko, D. L. (2006). Self-esteem in adolescent females. *Journal of Adolescent Health, 39,* 501–507.

Bronson, P., & Merryman, A. (2009). *NurtureShock: New thinking about children.* New York: Hachette Book Group.

Brown, L. M. (1998). *Raising their voices: The politics of girls' anger.* Cambridge, MA: Harvard University Press.

Brown, L. M. (2003). *Girlfighting: Betrayal and rejection among girls.* New York: New York University Press.

Catalyst. (2007). *The double-bind dilemma for women in leadership: Damned if you do, doomed if you don't.* New York: Author.

Centers for Disease Control and Prevention. (2007, July 09). *Web-based injury statistics query and reporting system* [online]. National Center for Injury Prevention and Control, Centers for Disease Control and Prevention. Retrieved from: www.cdc .gov/ncipc/wisqars/ default.htm

Centers for Disease Control and Prevention. (2012). *Youth risk behavior surveillance—United States 2011.* Washington, DC: Surveillance Summaries.

Chesler, P. (2009). *Women's inhumanity to women.* Chicago, IL: Lawrence Hill Books.

Child Welfare Information Gateway. (2012). *Sexual abuse indicators* [online]. U. S. Department of Health and Human Services, Administration for Children and Families. Retrieved from: http://www.childwelfare.gov/pubs/usermanuals/sexabuse/ sexabusec.cfm

Crick, N. R., & Grotpeter, J. K. (2005). Relational aggression, gender, and social-psychological adjustment. In M. Gauvain & M. Cole (Eds.). *Readings on the development of children* (4th ed.). New York, NY: Worth.

D'Antona, R., Kevorkian, M., & Russom, A. (2010). Sexting, texting, cyberbullying and keeping youth safe online. *Journal of Social Sciences, 6*(4), 521–526.

Davis-Keane, P. E. (2005). The influence of parent education and family income on child achievement: The indirect role of parental expectations and the home environment. *Journal of Family Psychology, 19*(2), 294–304.

Dichter, M. E., Cederbaum, J. A., & Teitelman, A. M. (2010). The gendering of violence in intimate relationships: How violence makes sex less safe for girls. In M. Chesney-Lind & N. Jones (Eds.), *Fighting for girls: New perspectives on gender and violence.* Albany: SUNY Press.

Eliot, L. (2009). *Pink brain, blue brain: How small differences grow into troublesome gaps—and what we can do about it.* Boston, MA: Houghton Mifflin Harcourt.

Fiebert, M. S. (1990). Dimensions of the female role. *Psychological Reports, 67*(2), 633–634.

Ford, H. H., Schindler, C. B., & Medway, F. J. (2001). School professionals' attributions of blame for child sexual abuse. *Journal of School Psychology, 39*(1), 25–44.

Gender and Empowerment Unit. (2009). *Girls' leadership development: Lessons from the field,* Atlanta, GA: CARE USA.

Gilligan, C. (1982). *In a different voice: Psychological theory and women's development.* Cambridge, MA: Harvard University Press.

Girl Scouts of the USA. (2008). *Change it up! What girls say about redefining leadership.* New York, NY: Girl Scout Research Institute.

Gottfredson, L. (1997). Assessing gender-based circumscription of occupational aspirations. *Journal of Career Assessment, 5*(4), 419–441.

Gottfredson, L. (2002). Gottfredson's theory of circumscription, compromise, and self-creation. In Brown, D. (Ed.), *Career choice and development.* San Francisco, CA: Jossey-Bass.

Grotpeter, J. K., & Crick, N. R. (1996). Relational aggression, overt aggression, and friendship. *Child Development, 67*(5), 2328–2338.

Hinkelman, L., & Bruno, M. (2008). The identification and reporting of child sexual abuse: The role of elementary school professionals. *Elementary School Journal, 108*(5), 376–391.

Hinkelman, L., & Sears, S. (2009). SASS-E Girlz: Giving girls the skills, attitudes, smarts, and science for engineering. *SASS-E Girlz Lesson Plan Package.* Chicago, IL: The Society of Women Engineers.

Kaukinen, C., Gover, A. R., & Hartman, J. L. (2011). College women's experiences of dating violence in casual and exclusive relationships. *American Journal of Criminal Justice, 37*(2), 146–162.

Knobloch-Westerwick, S., & Crane, J. (2012). A losing battle: Effects of prolonged exposure to thin ideal images on dieting and body satisfaction. *Communication Research, 39*(1), 79-102.

Kutob, R. M., Senf, J. H., Crago, M., & Shisslak, C. M. (2010). Concurrent and longitudinal predictors of self-esteem in elementary and middle school girls. *Journal of School Health, 80*(5), 240–248.

Leaper, C., Farkas, T., & Brown, C. S. (2012). Adolescent girls' experiences and gender-related beliefs in relation to their motivation in math/science and English. *Journal of Youth and Adolescence, 41*(3), 269–282.

Lipkins, S., Levy, J. M., & Jerabkova, B. (2010). Sexting . . . is it all about power? Retrieved from Real Psychology website:

http://realpsychology.com/content/tools-life/sextingis-it-all-about-power

Madsen, S. (2008). *On Becoming A Woman Leader: Learning from the Experiences of University Presidents.* San Francisco, CA: Jossey-Bass, Inc.

McAlinden, A. M. (2006). 'Setting 'em up': Personal, familial and institutional grooming in the sexual abuse of children. *Social Legal Studies, 15*(3), 339–362.

Merrell, K. M., Buchanan, R., & Tran, O. K. (2006). Relational aggression in children and adolescents: A review with implications for school settings. *Psychology in the Schools, 43,* 345–360.

Ms. Foundation for Women (2000). *The new girls' movement: charting the path.* New York, NY: Author.

National Institutes of Health, National Institute of Child Health and Human Development. (2012). *Puberty: What are the signs of puberty?* Retrieved from http://www.nichd.nih.gov/health/topics/puberty.cfm

National Science Foundation. (2003). *New formulas for America's workforce: Girls in science and engineering.* Retrieved from www.nsf.gov/publications/pub_summ.jsp?ods_key=nsf03207

Oppliger, P. (2008). *Girls gone skank: The sexualization of girls in American culture,* Jefferson, NC: McFarland & Company.

Packard, B. W., & Nguyen, D. (2003). Science career-related possible selves of adolescent girls: A longitudinal study. *Journal of Career Development, 29*(4), 251-263.

Patchin, J. W., & Hinduja, S. (2012). *Cyberbullying prevention and response: Expert perspectives.* New York: Routledge.

Pipher, M. (1994). *Reviving Ophelia: Saving the selves of adolescent girls.* New York, NY: Penguin Group.

Raskausas, J., & Stoltz, A. D. (2004). Identifying and intervening in relational aggression. *The Journal of School Nursing, 20*(4), 209–215.

Remillard, A., & Lamb, S. (2005). Adolescent girls' coping with relational aggression. *Sex Roles, 53*(3–4), 221–229.

Sears, H. A., & Byers, E. S. (2010). Adolescent girls' and boys' experiences of psychologically, physically, and sexually aggressive behaviors in their dating relationships: Co-occurrence and emotional reaction. *Journal of Aggression, Maltreatment, & Trauma, 19,* 517–539.

Simmons, R. (2002). *Odd girl out: The hidden culture of aggression in girls.* New York, NY: Harcourt, Inc.

Simmons, R. (2009). *The curse of the good girl: Raising authentic girls with courage and confidence.* New York: The Penguin Press.

Skelton, C., Francis, B., & Read, B. (2010). "Brains before 'beauty'?" High achieving girls, school, and gender identities. *Educational Studies, 36*(2), 185–194.

Smith, P. H., White, J. W., & Holland, L. J. (2003). A longitudinal perspective on dating violence among adolescent and college-age women. *American Journal of Public Health, 93*(7), 1104–1109.

Starr, C. R., & Ferguson, G. M. (2012). Sexy dolls, sexy grade-schoolers? Media and maternal influences on young girls' self-sexualization. *Sex Roles, 67*(7-8), 463-476.

Tolman, D., Impett, E. A., Tracy, A. J., & Michael, A. (2006). Looking good, sounding good: Femininity ideology and adolescent girls' mental health. *Psychology of Women Quarterly, 30*(1), 85–95.

U.S. Department of Justice. (2000). *Sexual assault of young children as reported to law enforcement: Victim, incident, and offender characteristics.* Retrieved from http://bjs.ojp.usdoj.gov/content/pub/pdf/saycrle.pdf

U.S. Department of Labor. (2011, July). *Highlights of women's earnings in 2010.* U.S. Bureau of Labor Statistics. Available online: http://www.bls.gov/cps/cpswom2010.pdf

Veronneau, M., & Dishion, T. J. (2011). Middle school friendships and academic achievement in early adolescence: A longitudinal analysis. *Journal of Early Adolescence, 31*(1), 99–124.

Vernon, A. (2009). *Counseling children and adolescents* (4th ed.). Denver, CO: Love.

Walker, S., Sanci, L., & Temple-Smith, M. (2011). Sexting and young people: Experts' views. *Youth Studies Australia, 30*(4), 8–16.

Wasulkiw, L., Emms, A., Meuse, R, & Poirier, K. F. (2009). Are all models created equal? A content analysis of women in advertisements of fitness versus fashion magazines. *Body Image, 6*(2), 137–140.

Werner, N. E., & Grant, S. (2009). Mothers' cognitions about relational aggression: associations with discipline responses, children's normative beliefs, and peer competence. *Social Development, 18,* 77–98.

Wigfield, A., Battle, A., Keller, L. B., & Eccles, J. S. (2002). Sex differences in motivation, self-concept, career aspiration, and career choice: Implications for cognitive development. In A. McGillicuddy-De Lisi & R. De Lisi (Eds.), *Biology, society, and behavior: The development of sex differences in cognition*. Westport, CT: Ablex.

Young, E. L., Boye, A. E., Nelson, D. A. (2006). Relational aggression: understanding, identifying, and responding in schools. *Psychology in the Schools, 43*(3), 297–312.

Index

Pages followed by t or f indicate tables or figures

CORWIN
A SAGE Company

The Corwin logo—a raven striding across an open book—represents the union of courage and learning. Corwin is committed to improving education for all learners by publishing books and other professional development resources for those serving the field of PreK–12 education. By providing practical, hands-on materials, Corwin continues to carry out the promise of its motto: **"Helping Educators Do Their Work Better."**